"No Remedy but Continual Prayer"

"No Remedy but Continual Prayer"

—— *John Wesley's Theology and Practice of Prayer* ——

Mark Murphree

WIPF & STOCK · Eugene, Oregon

"NO REMEDY BUT CONTINUAL PRAYER"
John Wesley's Theology and Practice of Prayer

Copyright © 2025 Mark Murphree. All rights reserved. Except for brief quotations in critical publications or reviews, no part of this book may be reproduced in any manner without prior written permission from the publisher. Write: Permissions, Wipf and Stock Publishers, 199 W. 8th Ave., Suite 3, Eugene, OR 97401.

Wipf & Stock
An Imprint of Wipf and Stock Publishers
199 W. 8th Ave., Suite 3
Eugene, OR 97401

www.wipfandstock.com

PAPERBACK ISBN: 979-8-3852-4677-9
HARDCOVER ISBN: 979-8-3852-4678-6
EBOOK ISBN: 979-8-3852-4679-3

VERSION NUMBER 08/15/25

To my Dad

For everything you've done, and continue to do

Contents

1 Development of a Theology of Prayer | 1
2 Prayer and Salvation | 17
3 Trinitarian Dynamics of Prayer | 25
4 Prayer and the Means of Grace | 36
5 The Lord's Prayer | 53
6 Prayer with Forms and Without | 63
7 Prayer and Community | 82
8 Prayer in Practice | 95
9 Prayer and Supernatural Manifestations | 112
10 Prayer and Revival | 127
11 Prayer and Mystic Quietism | 139
12 Prayer and Christian Perfection | 148

Bibliography | 161

— 1 —

Development of a Theology of Prayer

JOHN WESLEY WAS ONE of the most notable religious figures of the eighteenth century. He was one of the leaders of the Evangelical Revival, an Anglican minister, and the founder of the Methodist movement. He was highly educated, having studied at Oxford, and knew several languages, including both Greek and Hebrew. Although he never wrote a systematic theology, his corpus of theological writing is extensive, consisting of sermons, hymns, journals, letters, pamphlets, and books. Throughout these works, as throughout his life, he continually spoke of the importance of prayer.

He was born on June 17, 1703, at the rectory in Epworth, North Lincolnshire, England. The theology and practice of prayer evident in his mature years developed from his instruction as a child, to his practices as a young man at Oxford University, through his experiences as a parish priest in Wroot and in Georgia, and finally in his evangelical awakening at Aldersgate.

The foundation for his theology of prayer was laid early in his life through his religious instruction as a child in the larger family life of his parents, Susanna and Samuel Wesley. Susanna Wesley was raised as a Dissenter[1] and converted to Anglicanism. As the wife of a poor clergyman

---

1. *Dissenter* was a collective term for Protestant groups that opposed various aspects of Anglicanism in the 1600s and 1700s. Puritans were one of the largest of these groups. Although comprehensive statements about the beliefs of Dissenters are hard to make, popular dissenting beliefs included believers' baptism, separation of church and state,

and the mother of nineteen children (ten of whom lived to adulthood), she was the primary person responsible for their education and the management of the household. All appearances suggest she was highly organized and efficient. Adam Clarke says of her, "She was a woman that lived by rule, she methodized and arranged everything so exactly, that to each operation she had a time, and time sufficient to transact all the business of the family."[2] She raised her children in a disciplined regime of prayer and Scripture reading.[3]

In a letter dated July 24, 1732, Susanna describes to John Wesley her practice of religious instruction for her children: "The children of this family were taught, as soon as they could speak, the Lord's Prayer, which they were made to say at rising and bed-time constantly; to which, as they grew bigger, were added a short prayer for their parents, and some Collects; a short Catechism, and some portions of Scripture, as their memories could bear."[4] Besides prayers, she also introduced them to the rhythm of the Christian week and how to behave properly in their religious observances. She says, "They were very early made to distinguish the Sabbath from other days; before they would well speak or go. They were as soon taught to be still at family prayers, and to ask a blessing immediately after, which they used to do by signs, before they would kneel or speak."[5] These practices rooted her children in the foundational habits of Christianity.

This disciplined routine was interrupted with a fire at the rectory in February 1709, which nearly took five-year-old John Wesley's life. It began in the middle of the night, when the roof somehow caught fire. By the time the family awakened, the roof had already largely burned through. The parents and the maid tried to hustle the children outside, but John Wesley was left behind in the confusion. As her husband was carrying the children to the garden, Susanna recalls, "We heard the child in the nursery cry out miserably for help, which extremely moved him, but his affliction was much increased when he had several times attempted the stairs, then on fire, and found it was impossible to get near him. He then

---

and alternative models of church government, as well as enthusiastic or fanatical expressions of the faith (claims to divine revelation, fulfillments of prophecy, etc.).

2. Clarke, *Memoirs*, 323.
3. Selleck, "Common Prayer," 65.
4. Susanna Wesley to John Wesley, July 24, 1732, 389. For John Wesley's mature views on the Lord's Prayer, see chapter 5 of this book.
5. Susanna Wesley to John Wesley, July 24, 1732, 389.

gave him for lost and, kneeling down, commended his soul to God and left him, as he thought, burning."[6]

The boy was saved at the last minute, however, by some neighbors, one of whom climbed up on the shoulders of another to reach the boy: "But the boy, seeing none came to his assistance and being frighted by the hanging of the chamber and his bed being on fire, climbed up to the casement, where he was presently spied by the men in the yard, who immediately got up and pulled him out just in that article of time that the roof fell and beat the chamber to the earth."[7] This was a pivotal experience in the life of John Wesley, who often later in life referred to himself, in the words of Zechariah, as "a brand plucked out of the burning."[8] Ever after this, he had a sense of God's hand on his life.

The fire destroyed the rectory completely, and most of the worldly goods the family owned. In the wake of it, the children were scattered to live temporarily with other families where discipline was much more lax than Susanna Wesley had enforced. This led her to redouble her efforts when the children were restored, as she recounts: "When the house was rebuilt, and the children all brought home, we entered upon a strict reform; and then was begun the custom of singing psalms at beginning and leaving school, morning and evening."[9] She paired up the children, oldest with the youngest (speaking) child, and the next oldest with the next youngest, for regular Bible reading. "At five o'clock . . . they read the Psalms for the day, and a chapter in the New Testament; as, in the morning, they were directed to read the Psalms and a chapter in the Old: After which they went to their private prayers, before they got their breakfast, or came into the family."[10] With this, religious discipline returned.

Samuel Wesley

Susanna Wesley was not the only parent of John Wesley with a strong prayer life. John Wesley's father, Samuel Wesley, was a man whose life was characterized by prayer. Samuel Wesley was raised as a Dissenter and schooled

---

6. Susanna Wesley, *Writings*, 67.
7. Susanna Wesley, *Writings*, 67.
8. Wesley, *Works* (Jackson) 2:309 (November 26, 1753).
9. Susanna Wesley to John Wesley, July 24, 1732, 391.
10. Susanna Wesley to John Wesley, July 24, 1732, 391.

in Dissenting academies.[11] When tasked to write a response to some anti-Dissent tracts, he began researching, and was convinced to renounce Dissent and become an Anglican.[12] At the time, he was about sixteen, and he soon entered Exeter College, Oxford and eventually became an Anglican priest.[13] As an Anglican, he was an orthodox and pious High Churchman.[14] Samuel Wesley's piety was marked, among other things, by a concern for prayer, and this certainly influenced John Wesley's own attitudes and practices toward prayer throughout his life.

As befitting an Anglican, Samuel Wesley was devoted to the Book of Common Prayer. His enthusiasm for it was clear even in the worst of situations. After being jailed for debts, he writes, "I have leave to read prayers every morning and afternoon here in the prison."[15] After he was released, he established family devotions structured according to the Book of Common Prayer. A decade later, Samuel Wesley recorded in passing that family prayers in the morning included "the confession, absolution, and prayers for the king and prince."[16]

Samuel Wesley's love for prayer was evident in other ways, as well. He was burdened for the lost around the world, and once proposed to Archbishop Sharp an extensive plan for a three-pronged outreach to Anglicans, Roman Catholics, and unbelievers in the East Indies.[17] Although his proposal to become a missionary did not come to pass, his later correspondence with James Oglethorpe, governor of the Georgia colony, reveals his heart. He lamented being too old to travel overseas to Georgia and evangelize the natives himself, and concludes, "However, I can still reach them with my prayers, which I am sure will never be wanting."[18] He wrote

---

11. Clarke, *Memoirs*, 82.

12. Adam Clarke quotes John Wesley, "Some severe invectives being written against the Dissenters, Mr. S. Wesley, being a young man of considerable talents, was pitched upon to answer them. This set him on a course of reading, which soon produced an effect very different from what had been intended. Instead of writing the wished-for answer, he himself conceived he saw reason to change his opinions; and actually formed a resolution to renounce the Dissenters, and attach himself to the Established Church." Clarke, *Memoirs*, 89. What the actual reasons were, Clarke does not record.

13. Clarke, *Memoirs*, 89.

14. Selleck, "Common Prayer," 63.

15. Clarke, *Memoirs*, 177.

16. Clarke, *Memoirs*, 206.

17. Clarke, *Memoirs*, 167–69. John Sharp was archbishop of York from 1691–1714.

18. Clarke, *Memoirs*, 269.

DEVELOPMENT OF A THEOLOGY OF PRAYER

Lyndal, his friend and a resident of Georgia: "And now, I have some little inquiries to make of your new country . . . Whether your Indians have the Lord's Prayer in their own language?"[19]

In 1699, Samuel Wesley published his "Letter Concerning Religious Societies," a defense of religious societies, grassroots groups devoted to personal piety, which later formed the organizational basis for his sons John and Charles Wesley's Methodist Societies. One of the distinguishing characteristics of these societies that he singled out for accolade was their focus on prayer. In this letter, Samuel describes religious societies in the words of the ancients: "They often meet together . . . to pray and sing hymns to Christ as God."[20] He saw them as inheriting the tradition of "the exemplary piety of the old British monks" who "wrought honestly for their livings, and only met together at the hours of prayer."[21] He compared them favorably to similar societies founded by Monsieur de Renty among the tradesmen in France, whom Renty taught "constantly to go to prayers, sing psalms, read books of devotion, and discourse of their spiritual concerns one with another."[22] He answered the accusation that they were schismatics by saying he cannot see how there can "possibly be any occasion of schism . . . where one of the very bonds of the society is the constant frequenting of public prayers and communions."[23] The presence of prayer made religious societies valuable.

When Samuel's son John was at Oxford, Samuel was no doubt pleased to hear that John was considering taking orders. He wrote him back, saying that one who was considering taking holy orders "should take all the care he possibly can, with the advice of wiser and elder men—especially imploring with all humility, sincerity, and intention of mind, and with fasting and prayer, the direction and assistance of Almighty God, and his Holy Spirit, to qualify and prepare him for it."[24] When John and Charles came under fire for the Holy Club they had established at Oxford, Samuel wrote to encourage them: "I have the highest reason to bless God that He has given me two sons together in Oxford to whom He has given grace and courage to turn

---

19. Clarke, *Memoirs*, 270.
20. Clarke, *Memoirs*, 125.
21. Clarke, *Memoirs*, 126.
22. Clarke, *Memoirs*, 129. Jean Baptise de Renty (1611–1649) was a French aristocrat who became a lay leader in the church.
23. Clarke, *Memoirs*, 130.
24. Samuel Wesley Sr. to John Wesley, January 26, 1725, 7.

the war against the world and the devil, which is the best way to conquer them."[25] He follows this encouragement with an exhortation: "They have but one more enemy to combat with, the flesh; which if they take care to subdue by fasting and prayer, there will be no more for them to do but to proceed steadily in the same course, and expect the crown which fadeth not away."[26] Later, in the same letter, he continues, "Walk as prudently as you can, though not fearfully, and my heart and prayers are with you."[27] He not only encouraged prayer, but offered it freely.

Samuel Wesley's letters to his son John frequently request or offer prayer: "If you love yourself or me, pray heartily!"[28] "Pray hard, and watch hard."[29] "Fast, watch and pray, believe, love and endure, and be happy. Towards which you shall never want the most ardent prayers of [y]our affectionate father."[30] At the close of his life, he wrote his eldest son, Samuel: "I hinted at one thing, which I mentioned in my letter to your brother, whereon I depend more than upon all my own simple reasoning, and that is, earnest prayer to Him who smiles at the strongest resolutions of mortals, and can, in a moment, change or demolish them."[31]

Samuel and Susanna Wesley's examples and teachings strongly influenced their son John Wesley both in his formative years and throughout his life. Many of the attitudes and ideas present in his thinking on prayer later in life owe their genesis to the religious instruction he received at the hands of his father and mother. This largely consisted of the "Anglican prayers, the Psalter, the Collects, the Lord's Prayer, and the Scriptures" which all played a "daily role in the family's devotion and education."[32] "From the Epworth routine John Wesley developed the pattern both for his own personal devotion and for the Methodist societies. Discipline was seen as a key factor; the inner life was sustained by a genuine and regulated prayer life."[33] This discipline in prayer would be the foundation of his spiritual life once he left for college.

25. Samuel Wesley Sr. to John Wesley, September 28, 1730, 125.
26. Samuel Wesley Sr. to John Wesley, September 28, 1730, 125.
27. Samuel Wesley Sr. to John Wesley, September 28, 1730, 126.
28. Samuel Wesley Sr. to John Wesley, March 17, 1725, 13.
29. Samuel Wesley Sr. to John Wesley, July 14, 1725, 21.
30. Samuel Wesley Sr. to John Wesley, September 7, 1725, 33.
31. Clarke, *Memoirs*, 274.
32. Selleck, "Common Prayer," 66.
33. Selleck, "Common Prayer," 67.

Oxford

John Wesley matriculated at Christ Church College, Oxford, in the summer of 1720. There, his understanding of prayer and the spiritual life was deeply influenced by his readings of Thomas à Kempis's *Christian Pattern* (also known as *The Imitation of Christ*) and Jeremy Taylor's *Rules for Holy Living*.

At the behest of a friend, John Wesley read Jeremy Taylor. Several things troubled him in Taylor's book, particularly his understanding of humility and assurance of forgiveness. Taylor's views on humility and assurance bothered Wesley enough that he twice wrote home to his mother Susanna to ask her insight. However, these difficulties only highlight how powerfully the book was affecting him. Forty years later, in his letter to John Newton, he testifies to its role in awakening him spiritually: "In 1725 I met with Bishop Taylor's *Rules of Holy Living and Dying*. I was struck particularly with the chapter upon Intention, and felt a fixed intention to *give myself up to God*."[34] In Brian Selleck's evaluation, "Taylor's insistence upon daily self-examination and his affirmation of forms of prayer and frequent communion added dimension to Wesley's already existing scheme of general rules for governing his life."[35]

Shortly thereafter, Wesley read Kempis, which reinforced the direction Taylor had given to his spiritual life, especially his intention to give himself up to God. "In this I was much confirmed soon after by the *Christian Pattern*, and longed to *give God all my heart*. This is just what I mean by Perfection now: I sought after it from that very hour."[36] Much like Taylor, Kempis challenged Wesley to a deeper Christian life, and much like his reaction to Taylor, Wesley had some difficulties with some of Kempis's ideas. One idea that particularly bothered Wesley was Kempis's belief that "all mirth is vain and useless, if not sinful,"[37] which Wesley also wrote to his mother about, asking her insight. In her response to her son, Susanna Wesley writes back, "I take Kempis to have been an honest, weak man, that had more zeal than knowledge, by his condemning all mirth or pleasure as sinful or useless, in opposition to so many direct and plain texts of Scripture."[38] In addition, Wesley's father also responded, writing in support of Kempis

---

34. Wesley to John Newton, May 14, 1765, 298.
35. Selleck, "Common Prayer," 67.
36. Wesley to John Newton, May 14, 1765, 298–99.
37. Wesley to Mrs. Susanna Wesley, May 28, 1725, 16.
38. Susanna Wesley to John Wesley, June 8, 1725, 19.

and encouraging Wesley to take him seriously: "I've only this to add of my friend and old companion T. Kempis: that making a pretty many grains of allowance he may be read to great advantage, and that notwithstanding all his superstition and enthusiasm, 'tis almost impossible to peruse him seriously without admiring and (I think) in some measure imitating his heroic strains of humility, piety, and devotion."[39]

Even if some passages bothered John Wesley, he writes, "Yet I had frequently much sensible comfort in reading him, such as I was stranger to before."[40] One of the things that comforted him was a deeper understanding of religion. "I began to see, that true religion was seated in the heart," he says, "and that God's law extended to all our thoughts as well as words and actions."[41] Comforting though it was, it also spurred Wesley into life-changing religious resolutions, and these resolutions included a renewed emphasis on prayer. "I began to alter the whole form of my conversation and to set in earnest upon a new life. I set apart an hour or two a day for religious retirement. I communicated every week. I watched against all sins, whether in word or deed. I began to aim at, and pray for, inward holiness."[42] Unfortunately, as he recognized later in his life, "doing so much and living so good a life,' I doubted not but I was a good Christian."[43] In his book *Mysticism in the Wesleyan Tradition* Robert G. Tuttle Jr. argues that Kempis was "at the door of Wesley's mystical quest where he would become preoccupied (if not obsessed) with internal 'works-righteousness' (prayer and meditation as opposed to external action) as the means of salvation."[44] This becomes especially evident in his practices over the next few years.

Wesley was made a fellow of Lincoln College in 1725 and was ordained a deacon later that same year. During this time "early rising, endless resolutions, self-examination, fasting, ejaculatory prayers, and many other mystical means of purging the soul became common practice."[45] He left Oxford in 1727 to serve as a curate for his father in Wroot, which he did for a little over two years, and was ordained as a priest partway through his tenure in 1728. Around this time he read William Law's *Christian Perfection* and

39. Samuel Wesley Sr. to John Wesley, July 14, 1725, 21.
40. Wesley, *Works* (Jackson) 1:99 (May 24, 1738).
41. Wesley, *Works* (Jackson) 1:99 (May 24, 1738).
42. Wesley, *Works* (Jackson) 1:99 (May 24, 1738).
43. Wesley, *Works* (Jackson) 1:99 (May 24, 1738).
44. Tuttle, *Mysticism*, 62.
45. Tuttle, *Mysticism*, 68.

Serious Call, which convinced him to be even "more explicitly resolved to be *all devoted to God* in body, soul, and spirit,"[46] as well as some of the works of Francis Fenelon, including *Discourse on Simplicity*, which he transcribed in February 1727 for a friend.[47] Wesley's time in Wroot was extremely solitary, not only because of its size (three hundred residents) and isolation (nearly five miles from Epworth), but because Wesley chose to spend much time in solitary religious pursuits. Only a few months before he began his curacy, his letter to his mother states, "I should prefer, at least for some time, such a retirement as would seclude me from all the world, to the station I am now in."[48] This retirement lasted for practically the entire time he was at Wroot. Tuttle writes, "Wesley performed his pastoral duties with punctiliousness, but most of his effort during these two years would be spent in sorting out his own spiritual life."[49] His retirement ended when a "serious man" challenged him on the path he was taking: "Sir, you wish to serve God and go to heaven. Remember that you cannot serve Him alone. You must therefore find companions or make them; the Bible knows nothing of solitary religion."[50] Shortly thereafter, he was recalled to Oxford.

Once he returned to Oxford in 1729, he joined the Holy Club that his brother Charles Wesley and two others had formed. These four devoted themselves to deeds of piety and philanthropy, and John Wesley soon became their leader. They visited the prisons and helped both the poor and the sick.[51] Their prayer life was intense and disciplined. They "spent an hour every morning and evening in private prayer. They prayed upon entering or leaving church. They prayed 'in concert' (at the same time but separately) three times a week. They used ejaculations for humility, faith, hope, and love. Every day at 9, 12, and 3, they used a collect. Each opened and closed his meals with a grace."[52] But like their works of piety, their prayers were also thoughtful of others: "They interceded for friends on Sundays, for pupils on Mondays, for those who asked for it on Wednesdays and Fridays, and every day for the family with whom they lodged."[53]

---

46. Wesley to John Newton, May 14, 1765, 299.
47. Tuttle, *Mysticism*, 68.
48. Wesley to Mrs. Susanna Wesley, March 19, 1727, 42.
49. Tuttle, *Mysticism*, 72.
50. Moore, *Life*, 96.
51. Wesley, *Works* (Jackson) 1:99 (May 24, 1738).
52. Selleck, "Common Prayer," 70–71.
53. Selleck, "Common Prayer," 71.

His discipline of prayer worked well in the environment of Oxford. He would learn much from the testing of it overseas in the colony of Georgia, where his experiences and the people he encountered would introduce him to new sources for his theology of prayer.

Georgia

On Tuesday, October 21, 1735, John Wesley (along with his brother Charles Wesley and two friends) sailed from the harbor at Gravesend toward a new life in the colony of Georgia. He had been invited by James Oglethorpe, an old friend of his father's and the governor of the colony. Although he was going to be the priest for the Savannah colonists and his desire was to carry out a mission among the Native Americans, by his own admission his "chief motive, to which all the rest are subordinate, is the hope of saving my own soul."[54] By this measure, his time in Savannah ultimately ended in failure.

On the way over, Wesley and his companions kept strict schedules. In the mornings they rose at four, prayed privately for an hour, then read the Bible together for two hours, ate breakfast at seven, and had public prayers at eight. In the afternoons, they had evening prayer at four, private prayer from five to six, met together at eight for mutual exhortation, and retired to bed between nine and ten.[55] Throughout the voyage, Wesley was impressed by the behavior of a group of German Moravians who demonstrated humility, meekness, and service to the other passengers. This regard only increased after a frightening incident: "In the midst of the psalm wherewith their service began, the sea broke over, split the main-sail in pieces, covered the ship, and poured in between the decks, as if the great deep had already swallowed us up. A terrible screaming began among the English. The Germans calmly sung on."[56] The Moravians would prove to have a lasting impact on Wesley's spirituality.

Once in Georgia, his desired mission to the indigenous peoples never came to fruition, as he quickly became burdened with the weight of parish duties in Savannah. Part of this was his own strict following of the services in the Book of Common Prayer. He had two services a day before noon, expected attendance at weekly Communion, demanded adherence to precise baptismal protocol, and implemented days of fasting. Parishioners who

---

54. Wesley to John Burton, October 10, 1735, 188.
55. Wesley, *Works* (Jackson) 1:17–18 (October 21, 1735).
56. Wesley, *Works* (Jackson) 1:22 (January 25, 1736).

violated these were excluded from Communion.⁵⁷ His strictness alienated him from his congregation. Moreover, he took the opportunity afforded by his position as rector of a new colony in a new land to adjust the prescribed Anglican liturgy to suit his own taste and ideals. Generally, he adjusted the liturgy in the direction of the original 1549 edition of the Book of Common Prayer or for overall simplification. Selleck writes that he "updated those prayers in the prayer book pertaining to the royal family."⁵⁸ Wesley himself noted that he "began dividing the public prayers, according to the original appointment of the church."⁵⁹ He "shortened the daily services considerably. He omitted the opening scriptural sentences and the confessional sequence. He also dropped the last five prayers"⁶⁰ and used the 1549 version of the daily services, which he justified by its shorter prayers interfering less with "the rigorous routine of colonial life."⁶¹ All of these changes annoyed his parishioners, who eventually brought a formal grievance against him, accusing him of various irregularities and innovations in worship.⁶²

However, Wesley's public religious duties were only part of his spiritual life. Almost as soon as he arrived, he began a relationship with August Spangenberg, a leader of the Moravians in Georgia. Spangenberg encouraged him in his readings of the mystics, and the two frequently discussed the mystical writers. The most important long-term influence Spangenberg had on Wesley, though, was in his insistence on the assurance of salvation. The very first day they met, Spangenberg asked him, "Does the Spirit of God bear witness with your spirit, that you are a child of God?" Wesley was speechless. Spangenberg pressed again, asking, "Do you know Jesus Christ?" Wesley gathered himself to answer, somewhat noncommittally, "I know he is the Savior of the world." Spangenberg pressed him a third time, asking, "Do you know he has saved you?" Wesley replied, "I hope he has died to save me." Spangenberg continued to press him, asking, "Do you know yourself?" Wesley recalls his reply, "I said, 'I do.' But I fear they were vain words."⁶³

---

57. Selleck, "Common Prayer," 77.
58. Selleck, "Common Prayer," 74.
59. Wesley, *Works* (Jackson) 1:31 (May 9, 1736).
60. Selleck, "Common Prayer," 76.
61. Selleck, "Common Prayer," 76.
62. Wesley, *Works* (Jackson) 1:56–57 (September 1, 1737).
63. Wesley, *Works* (Jackson) 1:23 (February 7, 1736).

The seed Spangenberg planted regarding the importance of assurance of salvation was slow to germinate fully; in the meantime, Wesley was exploring the mystical approach to religion. By the end of 1736, he felt the failure of his mystical experiments. He wrote to his brother Samuel Wesley Jr. that November 23: "I think the rock on which I had the nearest made shipwreck of the faith was the writings of the Mystics."[64] The fundamental flaw in the mystical approach, he thought at this time, was its Quietism. "Public prayer, or any forms, they need not; for they pray without ceasing. Sensible devotion in any prayer they despise, it being a great hindrance to perfection."[65]

By the next year, Wesley had abandoned the reading of some of the mystical writers, but still read Kempis and Francke.[66] On January 2, he visited the Scottish immigrants at Darien, where he "was surprised to hear an extemporary prayer."[67] His initial reaction was resoundingly negative. "Are not then the words we speak to God to be set in order at least as carefully as those we speak to our fellow worms? One consequence of this manner of praying is, that they have public service only once a week. Alas, my brethren! I bear you record, ye have a zeal for God, but not according to knowledge."[68] His colleagues were more willing to try new things, however. Wesley records in his diary that at their prayers that evening, his close friend Benjamin Ingham "prayed extempore!"[69]

His relationships with his parishioners continued to deteriorate, including a romance with Sophia Hopkey, the niece of Savannah's chief magistrate, that ended bitterly. Eventually the Savannah colonists brought grievances against him. He decided he could do no more good there and returned home. His journal of Friday, December 2, 1737, reads, "I shook off the dust of my feet, and left Georgia, after having preached the gospel (not as I ought, but as I was able) one year, and nearly nine months."[70] His spiritual quest would continue, just not in the New World.

64. Wesley to Samuel Wesley Jr., November 23, 1736, 207.
65. Wesley to Samuel Wesley Jr., November 23, 1736, 208.
66. Tuttle, *Mysticism*, 90.
67. Wesley, *Journal* (Curnock) 309 (January 2, 1737).
68. Wesley, *Journal* (Curnock) 309–10 (January 2, 1737).
69. Wesley, *Journal* (Curnock) 309 (January 2, 1737). Curnock's edition of Wesley's *Journal* records, "I prayed extempore!" on this date. The *Bicentennial Edition*, however, which is generally considered authoritative, reads, "Ingham prayed extempore!" (Wesley, *Works* (Bicentennial) 18:460).
70. Wesley, *Works* (Jackson) 1:61 (December 2, 1737).

Aldersgate

While his mission to Georgia appeared to be an abject failure, Wesley had made a number of advances in his understanding of prayer and the spiritual life. Nor was his development to stagnate upon his return to England. He arrived back on February 1, 1738, and within a week, he encountered Peter Böhler, a Moravian. Böhler was vital to Wesley's spiritual journey toward his conversion at Aldersgate. Böhler and Wesley had a similar concern for holiness, but for Böhler, holiness "was the *fruit* of faith, not the *cause*."[71] Instead, Böhler preached justification by faith. As strange as it may seem, John Wesley, a priest in a Protestant church, had never heard the Reformation doctrine of justification by faith. Nearly a decade later, in his letter dated July 31, 1747, John Wesley wrote his brother Charles, "Some years ago we heard nothing about either justifying faith or a sense of pardon: so that, when we did hear of them, the theme was quite new to us."[72] John Wesley realized he did not have this faith, but took Böhler's advice to "Preach faith *till* you have it; and then, *because* you have it, you *will* preach faith."[73]

Wesley's shifting ideas seemed to accompany a relaxing of his bias toward ritual, especially in prayer. On Monday, March 27, 1738, he went with a friend to the Castle to minister to a condemned prisoner. After reading prayers and preaching, "we prayed with the condemned man, first in several forms of prayer, and then in such words as were given us in that hour."[74] The results were dramatic: "After a space he rose up, and eagerly said, 'I am now ready to die. I know Christ has taken away my sins; and there is no more condemnation for me.'"[75] Praying extempore as needed quickly became what Selleck calls a "liturgical principle" for Wesley.[76] In his very next journal entry, Wesley wrote, "My heart was so full that I could not confine myself to the forms of prayer which we were accustomed to use there. Neither do I purpose to be confined to them any more; but to pray indifferently, with a form or without, as I may find suitable to particular occasions."[77]

---

71. Tuttle, *Mysticism*, 104.
72. Wesley to Charles Wesley, July 31, 1747, 108.
73. Wesley, *Works* (Jackson) 1:86 (March 4, 1738).
74. Wesley, *Works* (Jackson) 1:90 (March 27, 1738).
75. Wesley, *Works* (Jackson) 1:90 (March 27, 1738).
76. Selleck, "Common Prayer," 81.
77. Wesley, *Works* (Jackson) 1:90 (April 1, 1738).

By April, he could write, "I had now no objection to what he said of the nature of faith; namely, that it is (to use the words of our Church) 'a sure trust and confidence which a man hath in God, that through the merits of Christ his sins are forgiven, and he reconciled to the favor of God.'"[78] Nevertheless, he still had problems coming to terms with the idea that this work was instantaneous, which was eventually overcome by both biblical investigation and the testimony of several people who had experienced this faith.[79] At this point, he resolved to seek this justifying faith "by absolutely renouncing all dependence, in whole or in part, upon *my own* works or righteousness . . . [and] by adding to the constant use of all the other means of grace, continual prayer for this very thing."[80] His seeking would soon bear fruit.

On May 4, Peter Böhler left to go overseas, leaving Wesley to work out this doctrine on his own. Wesley, however, was primed and ready. After spending the night of Saturday, May 20, in prayer, he received the "surprising news" that his brother Charles had experienced justification by faith.[81] The following Monday, Tuesday, and Wednesday John Wesley felt "continual sorrow and heaviness"[82] in his heart from the weight of his sins and the recognition that "all my works, my righteousness, my prayers, need an atonement for themselves."[83] All of these experiences came to a head on the evening of May 24, 1738. Wesley recounts,

> In the evening I went very unwillingly to a society in Aldersgate-Street, where one was reading Luther's preface to the Epistle to the Romans. About a quarter before nine, while he was describing the change which God works in the heart through faith in Christ, I felt my heart strangely warmed. I felt I did trust in Christ, Christ alone for salvation: And an assurance was given me, that he had taken away *my* sins, even *mine*, and saved *me* from the law of sin and death.[84]

The effect of this was seen immediately in prayer, as that was John Wesley's first response to his experience. As he relates, "I began to pray with

78. Wesley, *Works* (Jackson) 1:90 (April 22, 1738).
79. Wesley, *Works* (Jackson) 1:91 (April 22, 1738).
80. Wesley, *Works* (Jackson) 1:102 (May 24, 1738).
81. Wesley, *Works* (Jackson) 1:96 (May 20, 1738).
82. Wesley, *Works* (Jackson) 1:97 (May 20, 1738).
83. Wesley, *Works* (Jackson) 1:97 (May 20, 1738).
84. Wesley, *Works* (Jackson) 1:103 (May 24, 1738).

all my might for those who had in a more especial manner despitefully used me and persecuted me."[85] Over the next few days, he experienced peace, but not joy, such that by Saturday, May 27, he writes, "Believing one reason of my want of joy was want of time for prayer, I resolved to do no business till I went to church in the morning, but to continue pouring out my heart before Him."[86] On Wednesday, May 31, Wesley wrote that he grieved "the Spirit of God, not only by not *watching unto prayer*, but likewise by speaking with sharpness instead of tender love . . . it pleased God, while I was exhorting another, to give comfort to my soul, and (after I had spent some time in prayer) to direct me to those gracious words"[87] of consolation found in Heb 10, "Having therefore boldness to enter into the holiest by the blood of Jesus, let us draw near with a true heart in full assurance of faith. Let us hold fast the profession of our faith without wavering; (for He is faithful that promised;) and let us consider one another to provoke unto love and good works."[88] From this point on, Wesley's life is no longer an account of spiritual searching, but of a working out of the implications of what he has found.

Conclusion

By the time he turned thirty-five in 1738, John Wesley was a broadly experienced minister. He had ministered in the ivory tower of Oxford, the small parish of Wroot, and the colony of Georgia. In the process, he had experienced his share of failure: a nonexistent missionary enterprise among the Native Americans, a failed romance, and strained relationships with his parishioners in Savannah.

Through it all, he had explored several different avenues of Christian spirituality. He had been High Church, focused on external works, focused on internal works, mystical, and now finally evangelical. Each of these approaches left an imprint on his theology and practice of prayer. Mysticism, especially, although he had made a break with its fundamental tenets, continued to influence him, as attested by his abridgments of mystical writers included in his *Christian Library*. Although later encounters and experiences would also influence him, Wesley had at this point answered

---

85. Wesley, *Works* (Jackson) 1:103 (May 24, 1738).
86. Wesley, *Works* (Jackson) 1:104 (May 27, 1738).
87. Wesley, *Works* (Jackson) 1:105 (May 31, 1738).
88. Wesley, *Works* (Jackson) 1:105 (May 31, 1738).

his major theological questions and searched for and found the assurance of salvation. From this point on, his theology is set enough that one may talk about his theology and practice, of prayer or anything else.

— 2 —

Prayer and Salvation

UNDERSTANDING PRAYER IN JOHN Wesley's theology as the ground or foundation of the Christian life properly begins in understanding the role of prayer in salvation. Wesley conceived of salvation in four major steps: prevenient grace, repentance, justification, and sanctification[1] and considered prayer to have an important role in all four. This chapter begins by examining the nature of prevenient grace and its role in prayer, especially prayers of unbelievers. Next, it looks at the role prayer plays in repentance and justification. Finally, this chapter explores the place of prayer in sanctification.

Prayer and Prevenient Grace

From time to time, Wesley's theology (and Arminian theology in general) has been accused of being a "human-centered" religion. That is, the focus of Wesley's theology (it is alleged) is on what humanity does rather than what God accomplishes in his sovereignty. For instance, the noted Reformed theologian and author James Montgomery Boice wrote that Arminians "are focused on [themselves] and . . . are in love with their own supposed spiritual abilities."[2]

---

1. Wesley, "Sermon 85," 509.
2. Boice, *Grace*, 168.

Likewise, Southern Baptist Theological Seminary president Al Mohler wrote of the "human-centered focus of the Arminian tradition."[3]

Properly understood, however, Wesley's Arminian theology is not human centered at all. In and of oneself, Wesley writes, a human has an "utter inability to do any good," and this reveals "the absolute necessity of the grace and Spirit of God to raise even a good thought or desire in our hearts."[4] Whatever a human does, it is only on the basis of God's prior, prevenient grace that he or she is able to do it, and this includes prayer. Even the most casual prayers of believers are only possible because of the overwhelming amount of grace that brought them to such a point in their lives that they can and would turn to God with their needs. Thomas Oden calls this "the fourfold sequence of the work of saving grace," consisting of prevenient grace, convincing grace, justifying grace, and sanctifying grace.[5]

Although the word *prevenient* simply means "prior," Wesley used it specifically to refer to the grace that brought people to an awareness of their need for salvation. Oden defines prevenient grace in the writings of Wesley as "the grace that begins to enable one to choose further to cooperate with saving grace."[6] Wesley states it this way: "Salvation begins with what is usually termed (and very properly) *preventing grace*; including the first wish to please God, the first dawn of light concerning his will, and the first slight transient conviction of having sinned against him."[7] Although this is not the fullness of saving grace, Wesley says, "All these imply some tendency toward life; some degree of salvation; the beginning of a deliverance from a blind, unfeeling heart, quite insensible of God and the things of God."[8] Some might suggest that this is but the action of conscience, a natural part of the makeup of all healthy people. Wesley was quick to clarify this misunderstanding, ascribing it to prevenient (preventing) grace. He said, in one of his sermons, "Though in one sense [conscience] may be termed natural, because it is found in all men; yet, properly speaking it is not natural, but

---

3. Mohler, "Evangelical," 34. These two examples are taken from a long list of examples in Olson, "Arminianism."

4. Wesley to John Fletcher, March 22, 1771, 231.

5. Oden, *Scriptural Christianity*, 246.

6. Oden, *Scriptural Christianity*, 243.

7. Wesley, "Sermon 85," 509.

8. Wesley, "Sermon 85," 509.

a supernatural gift of God . . . which we usually style, preventing grace."[9] Elsewhere, he addressed the same issue, writing, "No man living is entirely destitute of what is vulgarly called *natural conscience*. But this is not natural: It is more properly termed, *preventing grace*."[10]

Prayers of Unbelievers

In 1665, the English Puritan Thomas Brooks wrote, "He that makes God the object of closet-prayer, but not the end of closet-prayer, doth but lose his prayer, and take pains to undo himself. . . . A man's most glorious actions will at last be found to be but glorious sins, if he hath made himself, and not the glory of God, the end of those actions."[11] He was expressing an idea, poplar among Reformed theologians (and often ascribed to Augustine) that "good works" done apart from the desire for God's glory, and thus the "good works" commonly ascribed to pagans, were but *splendida peccata*—"splendid sins."[12] Wesley strongly objected to this idea that all acts one does before salvation, including prayer, are merely splendid sins. The case of Cornelius in Acts 10 provided a precedent for him. In his commentary on Acts 10 in his *Explanatory Notes on the New Testament*, Wesley paid special attention to verse 4, which says, "Thy prayers and thine alms are come up for a memorial before God" and comments, "Dare any man say, These were only splendid sins? Or that they were an abomination before God? And yet it is certain, in the Christian sense Cornelius was then an unbeliever. He had not then faith in Christ."[13] This was grounds for Wesley to argue that prayer was not exclusively the province of the redeemed. He continues, "So certain it is, that every one who seeks faith in Christ, should seek it in prayer, and doing good to all men."[14] He understood that this was what Cornelius had been doing, for his comment on Acts 10:31, "Thy

---

9. Wesley, "Sermon 105," 187–89.
10. Wesley, "Sermon 85," 512.
11. Brooks, "Privy Key," 273–74.
12. Marshall cites the earliest occurrence of the phrase *splendida peccata* as Peter Martyr's summary of and inference from Augustine's *City of God*, found in Martyr's *Common Places*, published posthumously after Martyr's death in 1562. Marshall, "Queries," 87.
13. Wesley, *Explanatory Notes*, 302.
14. Wesley, *Explanatory Notes*, 302.

prayer is heard," reads, "Doubtless he had been praying for instruction, how to worship God in the most acceptable manner."[15]

Wesley rejected the idea that Cornelius was some sort of transitional figure whose conversion experience did not apply to later generations. In a letter, he responded to the question, "Ought every unbeliever to pray or communicate?" by answering, "Yes. 'Ask, and it (faith) shall be given you.' And if you believe Christ died for guilty, helpless sinners, then eat that Bread and drink of that Cup."[16] As Selleck put it, "In Wesley's schema the means of grace are not limited to the saved; they are open to those seeking salvation."[17] Wesley explained this more thoroughly in his journal:

> For God hath in Scripture ordained prayer, reading or hearing . . . as the ordinary means of conveying his grace to man. . . . For thus saith the Lord, "Ask, and it shall be given you. If any of you lack wisdom, let him ask of God." Here God plainly ordains prayer as the means of receiving whatsoever grace we want; particularly that wisdom from above, which is the chief fruit of the grace of God.
>
> Here, likewise, God commands all to pray who desire to receive any grace from him. Here is no restriction as to believers or unbelievers; but, least of all, as to unbelievers: For such, doubtless, were most of those to whom he said, "Ask, and it shall be given you."
>
> We know, indeed, that the prayer of an unbeliever is full of sin. Yet let him remember that which is written of one who could not then believe, for he had not so much as heard the Gospel, "Cornelius, thy prayers and thine alms are come up for a memorial before God."[18]

Selleck highlights this as one of Wesley's theological departures from the prevailing norm, designed to address the flaws he perceived in it: "Wesley's approach to the means of grace differs from the Anglican heritage. . . . All of the means convey God's grace to unbelievers as well as to believers. As a corrective to the rampant formalism of his day, which he believed mistook the means for the end, he tended to emphasize the inward spiritual end or grace over the outward means."[19] Even as he affirmed Cornelius as a praying unbeliever, Wesley still acknowledged a

---

15. Wesley, *Explanatory Notes*, 304.
16. Wesley to John Simpson, November 28, 1774, 124.
17. Selleck, "Common Prayer," 96.
18. Wesley, *Works* (Jackson) 1:278–79 (June 25, 1740).
19. Selleck, "Common Prayer," 309–10.

clear distinction between the prayers of believers and unbelievers. First, he refused to suggest that, even if not splendid sins, the prayers of unbelievers were meritorious in any respect. In fact, after calling for those who "seek faith in Christ" to do so in prayer, he cautions, "In strictness what is not exactly according to the Divine rule must stand in need of Divine favour and indulgence."[20] In other words, while not splendid sins, they did still qualify as sins in the broadest use of the term.

Wesley's approval of praying unbelievers might seem to contradict Scripture; in the case of Jesus's healing of the man born blind, the man testifies before the Sanhedrin that "we know that God heareth not sinners."[21] Wesley explains that this refers to "impenitent sinners, so as to answer their prayers in this manner."[22] The difference here is the attitude of heart. Although God clearly does answer the prayers of unbelieving seekers like Cornelius, the prayers of the impenitent are powerless and unavailing.

Perhaps most importantly, though, Wesley affirmed that true faith was required for all but the most basic levels of prayer. In a letter enumerating his disagreements with Ramsay's *Philosophical Principles of Natural and Revealed Religion*, he quotes Ramsay's statement, "Prayer, mortification, and self-denial produce necessarily in the soul faith, hope, and charity."[23] While on the surface this might sound similar to what Wesley himself has said, he disagreed with it forcefully, saying, "On the contrary, faith must necessarily precede both prayer, mortification, and self-denial, if we mean thereby 'adoring God in spirit and in truth, a continual death to all that is visible, and a constant, universal suppression and sacrifice of all the motions of false love.' And the Chevalier talks of all these like a mere parrot, if he did not know and feel in his inmost soul that it is absolutely false that any of these should subsist in our heart till we truly believe in the Son of God."[24] Taking Ramsay's own definition of prayer, "adoring God in spirit and in truth," Wesley denies that it is available to those without faith.

While prayer can precede faith in certain special cases, it cannot come before prevenient grace. Faith may come by asking in prayer, but prayer itself is a response to the stirring of God's prevenient grace. This is best illustrated by Wesley's comments on children's prayers: "Although there may

20. Wesley, *Explanatory Notes*, 302.
21. Wesley, *Explanatory Notes*, 242.
22. Wesley, *Explanatory Notes*, 242.
23. Wesley to Dr. John Robertson, September 24, 1753, 109.
24. Wesley to Dr. John Robertson, September 24, 1753, 110.

be some use in teaching even very young children to 'say their prayers daily,' yet I judge it to be utterly impossible to teach any to 'practise prayer' till they are awakened. For what is prayer but the desire of the soul expressed in words to God, either inwardly or outwardly? How then will you teach them to *express* a desire who *feel* no desire at all?"[25]

Prayer, Repentance, and Justification

Full conviction of sin that results in true repentance is the second stage in Wesley's conception of salvation. Wesley says, "Salvation is carried on by *convincing grace*, usually in Scripture termed *repentance*; which brings a larger measure of self-knowledge, and a farther deliverance from the heart of stone."[26] Harald Lindström calls this "properly, the first real step on the way to salvation."[27] The prayer of repentance, then, is a direct result of prior convincing grace. One might question whether such a distinction between prevenient grace and convincing grace is necessary, but Wesley thought it was. Many people have a conscience that bothers them when they do wrong but silence their thoughts and pursue it no further. Conscience is real (prevenient) grace, but they refuse to cooperate with it. Under the influence of convincing grace, however, they are convinced of their sins and of sin's undesirability. Convincing grace brings them to a point of repentance, where they can receive God's justifying grace.

The experience of convincing grace and repentance leads to justifying grace, the third in the sequence of saving grace. Wesley says, "Afterwards we experience the proper Christian salvation; whereby, 'through grace,' we 'are saved by faith;' consisting of those two grand branches, justification and sanctification. By justification we are saved from the guilt of sin, and restored to the favour of God."[28] This is salvation as the term is commonly used today when people speak of "getting saved" or "being saved." Through justification, God forgives and pardons the sinner, restoring his or her relationship with God. However, it is important to remember that Wesley considered justification to be only one of "two grand branches"[29] of "proper

---

25. Wesley to Philothea Briggs, September 8, 1773, 39.
26. Wesley, "Sermon 85," 509.
27. Lindström, *Sanctification*, 113.
28. Wesley, "Sermon 85," 509.
29. Wesley, "Sermon 85," 509.

Christian salvation";[30] he rejected the notion of any Christianity that did not result in transformed lives through the sanctifying power of the Spirit.

Prayer and Sanctification

Sanctifying grace is the fourth in the sequence of saving grace. Wesley says, "By sanctification we are saved from the power and root of sin, and restored to the image of God."[31] It is not enough to be saved from the guilt of sin; God's plan and provision is to deliver his people from the dominion and activity of sin, and in fact, he begins this immediately. "At the same time that we are justified, yea, in that very moment, sanctification begins. In that instant we are born again, born from above, born of the Spirit: There is a *real* as well as a *relative* change. We are inwardly renewed by the power of God."[32] The relative change to which Wesley refers is the change in status and relationship to God. The real change results in a transformed life, the substitution of godly thoughts and actions for ungodly ones. To this end, God has provided the Holy Spirit.

The presence of the Holy Spirit in the life of Christians is the wellspring of their sanctification. Through the Spirit, believers receive the witness of the Spirit, testifying of their status as children of God (Rom 8:16). Wesley identifies the "witness of the Spirit" as the assurance of God's love: "But we must love God, before we can be holy at all; this being the root of all holiness. Now we cannot love God, till we know he loves us. 'We love him, because he first loved us.' And we cannot know his pardoning love to us, till his Spirit witnesses it to our spirit."[33] Of this, Lindström writes, "The consciousness imparted through the testimony of the Holy Spirit that God loves man is a necessary condition of man loving God. This latter love, moreover, is the source of all sanctity in heart and life."[34] Sanctification is the outworking of love, given by God and received by humans, transforming them in the process.

The sanctifying work that this love of God initiates in the life of the believer includes all godly habits, including initiating the desire for prayer. "All which does not spring from this loving knowledge of God

30. Wesley, "Sermon 85," 509.
31. Wesley, "Sermon 85," 509.
32. Wesley, "Sermon 43," 45.
33. Wesley, "Sermon 10," 115.
34. Lindström, *Sanctification*, 115.

[is sin]; which knowledge cannot begin or subsist one moment without immediate inspiration; [including] all public worship, and all private prayer."[35] Lycurgus Starkey comments on this: "Any strong inclination of our spirit to public or private prayer is likewise recognized to be the movement of the Spirit."[36]

The question remains, however, how the Spirit moves in one's heart to direct one's actions, to pray or do any other activity. The Spirit's impulses are directive, but not compelling. One should consider such impulses as a "holy prompt," and not expect more powerful direction. Wesley considered the situation: "Here is a man ready to perish with hunger. How am I 'led by the Spirit' to relieve him? First, by His convincing me it is the will of God I should; and Secondly, by His filling my heart with love toward him. Both this light and this heat are the gift of God; are wrought in me by the same Spirit, who leads me, by this conviction as well as love, to go and feed that man."[37] In other words, both through the intellect and through the emotions, the Spirit delivers his directive prompts. For the Christian to say, "I am praying because it seems like a good idea to pray" is but to say, "The Spirit is prompting me through intellectual conviction to pray." Likewise, to say, "I am praying because I am moved by love and concern for the situation" is but to say, "I am moved emotionally by the Holy Spirit to pray."

Conclusion

Wesley saw the process of salvation as inextricably bound up with prayer. All prayer is a result of grace, and prevenient grace empowers individuals to pray, even if they are not yet believers. Wesley found scriptural support for the importance of unbelievers to pray and saw Cornelius as a model for that. Whatever dim awakening unbelievers experience that allows them to pray, this is not yet saving grace; for that, they must come under convincing grace, which allows them to actually repent. In response to repentance, God gives justifying grace, which saves unbelievers from damnation, and then sanctifying grace, which saves them from the dominion and activity of sin. Sanctification is carried out in believers through the Holy Spirit, who initiates the desire to pray in their hearts through the revelation of the love of God.

35. Wesley, *Farther Appeal, Part II*, 188.
36. Starkey, *Holy Spirit*, 72.
37. Wesley, *Farther Appeal, Part II*, 188.

— 3 —

Trinitarian Dynamics of Prayer

THE GROUND OF A Christian life is a relationship with God, which necessarily involves communication and interaction with him, of which prayer is a prime example. Prayer shapes and is shaped by one's theology, which is why the Trinitarian dynamics of prayer remain so important. The "how" and "why" of prayer always exist secondary to the "to whom" of prayer; the ins and outs of relational communication are always based on the person to whom one relates.

Prayer to God the Father is always, everywhere assumed by Wesley. This chapter will examine how prayer leads to the knowledge of God in Wesley's writings. Next, it will look at how Wesley addressed the question of God's impassibility, and how that interacted with one's expectation for answered prayer. Wesley argued for prayer to Christ, and supported prayer to the Holy Spirit, as well. Here, this chapter will show, Wesley drew the line and rejected prayers and invocations to any other beings, earthly or heavenly.

Prayer and the Knowledge of God

Wesley recognized that prayer and the knowledge of God were mutually reinforcing. He understood Paul to teach that one should pray for knowledge of God and his will. Paul's prayer in Phil 1:9, that the Philippians should abound in knowledge and all spiritual sense, was Wesley's cue to pray for this knowledge. He understood this spiritual sense to be "the ground of all spiritual knowledge. We must be inwardly sensible of divine peace, joy, love; otherwise, we cannot know what they are."[1] Likewise, Christians should pray for the knowledge of God's will, as Paul did for the Colossians, to the effect that through this spiritual understanding, one may "discern by that light whatever agrees with, or differs from, [God's] will."[2]

This knowledge of God results in increased prayer. In the day Jesus spoke of when he would "shew you plainly of the Father," the disciples would "ask in [his] name."[3] Wesley saw a direct correlation between this greater knowledge of God and increased prayer, commenting that "true knowledge begets prayer."[4]

Prayer and Impassibility

The first of the Thirty-Nine Articles of Religion in the Anglican Church says that God is "without body, parts, or passions,"[5] and Wesley spent his entire life as part of the Church of England. At various points in his *Notes on the New Testament*, he indicated that he understood scriptural discussion of God's passions to be anthropopathisms. For instance, in commenting on Luke 15:7, which speaks of joy in heaven, Wesley commented that God may be "represented as having part in that joy."[6] When Heb 3:10 states that God "was grieved," Wesley commented that this grief is only "to speak after the manner of men."[7] However, he adapted the Anglican Articles for the Methodists, and removed the phrase "or passions" by the 1788 edition.[8] Kenneth Collins explains that for Wesley, "God is not without passions, properly understood, in that holy love itself is a passion."[9] By removing the phrase, Wesley removed the possibility of a potentially serious misunderstanding.

---

1. Wesley, *Explanatory Notes*, 506.
2. Wesley, *Explanatory Notes*, 517.
3. Wesley, *Explanatory Notes*, 261.
4. Wesley, *Explanatory Notes*, 261.
5. Church of England, "Articles of Religion."
6. Wesley, *Explanatory Notes*, 182.
7. Wesley, *Explanatory Notes*, 570. I am indebted to Gregory S. Clapper for this insight (Clapper, *Affections*, 90–91).
8. Wesley, *Sunday Service*, 313.
9. Collins, *Theology*, 144.

With regard to prayer, the fundamental question of God's impassibility is related to whether prayer can change God's mind about a situation. Wesley said, "So that the end of your praying is not to inform God, as though he knew not your wants already; but rather to inform yourselves; to fix the sense of those wants more deeply in your hearts, and the sense of your continual dependence on Him who only is able to supply all your wants. It is not so much to move God, who is always more ready to give than you to ask, as to move yourselves, that you may be willing and ready to receive the good things he has prepared for you."[10] In this passage, Wesley affirms God's omniscience; prayer is not about informing God of details of which he was previously unaware. The more important point is that he also affirmed God's fundamental willingness to answer prayer—that, in fact, he is "more ready" to give than the reluctant person praying is to petition. Wesley seemed to indicate that changing God's mind (even if possible) is unnecessary; he is generously ready to act differently on account of one's prayer.

The obvious follow-up question, "Why, if God is so willing to grant us our requests, does he wait until Christians pray about them?" is also answered here. God waits for prayer to prepare the one who is praying to receive what he is going to give. That is, prayer is less about convincing a reluctant God to give, and more about a reluctant asker learning to admit weakness, neediness, and "continual dependence" on God.

Prayer and Christ as Prophet

The work of Christ is traditionally examined through his roles as Prophet, Priest, and King. Wesley's understanding of each of Christ's roles reveals how he viewed the relationship between Christ and prayer. As Prophet, Christ speaks to humanity the very words of God. Wesley highlights the importance of this role in his comments on the beginning of the Gospel of Matthew: "And with respect to ourselves, we find a total darkness, blindness, ignorance of God, and the things of God. Now here we want Christ in his prophetic office, to enlighten our minds, and teach us the whole will of God."[11]

When commenting on the beginning of the Sermon on the Mount, Wesley again emphasizes Christ's role as Prophet: "Let us observe, who it

10. Wesley, "Sermon 26," 332.
11. Wesley, *Explanatory Notes*, 11.

is that is here speaking. . . . It is the great Prophet of the Lord, concerning whom God had solemnly declared long ago, 'Whosoever will not hearken unto my words which he shall speak in my name, I will require it of him.'"[12]

In this role, Christ instructs his disciples how to pray, giving them the Lord's Prayer. Wesley's consciousness of Christ's role as Prophet clearly lies behind his comments on Matt 6:9, where he takes up the themes of humanity's blindness and ignorance in relation to prayer: "He who best knew what we ought to pray for, and how we ought to pray, what matter of desire, what manner of address would most please himself, would best become us, has here dictated to us a most perfect and universal form of prayer, comprehending all our real wants, expressing all our lawful desires; a complete directory and full exercise of all our devotions."[13] As the Prophet, Christ's instructions are God's words, and his teachings on prayer are full, complete, and perfect.

Prayer and Christ as Priest

The second role of Christ is that of Priest. The essence of Christ's priestly role is as mediator between God and humanity. In this role, Christ offered himself to God as an atoning sacrifice for the sins of humanity. Wesley summarizes the importance of this mediatorship in his comment on 1 Tim 2:5, "We could not rejoice that there is a God, were there not a Mediator also; one who stands between God and men, to reconcile man to God, and to transact the whole affair of our salvation."[14] Wesley clearly saw a relationship between Christ's "once for all" atonement and his continuing intercession. In fact, it is on the basis of Christ's atoning sacrifice that he continually offers intercession. When the author of Hebrews writes that he "ever lives to make intercession," Wesley explains, "He died once. He intercedes perpetually."[15] This relationship is perhaps most visible in Wesley's comments on Heb 10, where he said a human priest stands as "a servant in a humble posture,"[16] but that Christ intercedes as "a Son in majesty and

---

12. Wesley, "Sermon 21," 247–48.

13. Wesley, *Explanatory Notes*, 25. Further analysis of the Lord's Prayer is found in chapter 5 of this book.

14. Wesley, *Explanatory Notes*, 540.

15. Wesley, *Explanatory Notes*, 578.

16. Wesley, *Explanatory Notes*, 584.

honour"[17] and in his comment on John 17, "He asks, as having a right to be heard, and prays, not as a servant, but a Son."[18]

Selleck explains this relationship: "Christ's obedience as man's representative substitute is the ground . . . of Christ's heavenly intercession. On his priestly work our relationship with God depends."[19] That is, the current prayers of Christians as well as the intercessory prayers of Christ are built on the foundation of Christ's priestly work. Furthermore, "like atonement, intercession is founded in Christ's passion and death, the effects of which he took with him in his own body when he ascended into the presence of God, where the virtue of his sacrifice remains forever."[20] The Book of Common Prayer "sees an indissoluble relationship between that 'one sufficient sacrifice' and Christ's continuing intercession,"[21] and Wesley's own view reflected that perspective.

Wesley's understanding of Christ's role in prayer is inextricably tied to his office as the great High Priest described by the author of Hebrews. As Priest, his role in prayer is twofold: to present to the Father both his own prayers and the prayers of Christians. This is evident in Wesley's comment on Rom 1:8, "The gifts of God all pass through Christ to us; and all our petitions and thanksgivings pass through Christ to God."[22] Wesley saw this reality behind Paul's comment in Rom 8:34 about Jesus interceding for us, explaining that Jesus is "presenting there his obedience, his sufferings, his prayers, and our prayers sanctified through him."[23] Wesley saw Christ, in his Priestly role, to be the sole mediator between God and humanity, and this is especially true with respect to prayer.

Wesley understood incense to be an image of and symbol for prayer, and he interpreted Jesus's office as a High Priest in light of that. In his comment on Luke 1:10, Wesley writes, "Prayer is in Scripture so often compared to incense. Perhaps one reason of ordaining incense might be, to intimate the acceptableness of the prayer that accompanied it; as well as to remind the worshippers of that sacrifice of a sweet-smelling savour, which was once to be offered to God for them, and of that incense, which is continually

17. Wesley, *Explanatory Notes*, 584.
18. Wesley, *Explanatory Notes*, 264.
19. Selleck, "Common Prayer," 210.
20. Selleck, "Common Prayer," 210–11.
21. Selleck, "Common Prayer," 221–22.
22. Wesley, *Explanatory Notes*, 361.
23. Wesley, *Explanatory Notes*, 385.

offered with the prayers of the saints, upon the golden altar that is before the throne."[24] No doubt Wesley felt that this association was justified by Scripture. Wesley commented on Rev 5:8 that the bowls full of incense, "which are the prayers of the saints," were the prayers "of the other saints still upon earth, whose prayers were thus emblematically represented in heaven."[25] Later, in a comment on Rev 8:3, he says, "Incense generally signifies prayer . . . and there was much incense; for as the prayers of all the saints in heaven and earth are here joined together."[26]

Offering incense was the duty of the priests, and as the great High Priest, Jesus's offering of prayers (both his own and of Christians) was a fulfillment of this duty. This was foremost in Wesley's mind, as his comment on Heb 9:6 illustrates. When the author of Hebrews mentions that the priests in the earthly temple were "accomplishing their services," Wesley explained that this refers to four duties in particular: "lighting the lamps, changing the shewbread, burning incense, and sprinkling the blood of the sin offerings."[27]

In his role as Priest, Jesus acts as the mediator between God and humanity, having offered himself as a "once for all" atonement for the sins of his people. On the basis of this atonement, Jesus receives the prayers of the faithful and offers them to God, along with his own intercession. In his role as King, however, Jesus receives prayer directly.

Prayer and Christ as King

In his role as Prophet, Christ speaks the words of God more fully and truly than any previous prophet. In his role as Priest, Christ can represent the human race before the Father more perfectly than any previous High Priest. In his role as King, Christ most completely embodies his divinity as the ultimate Sovereign over all creation. It is this role that best exemplifies why humanity can pray, not only to the Father through the Son, but directly to the Son himself.

Wesley found numerous examples of scriptural support for praying to Jesus. He saw Stephen's death-prayer to Jesus to receive his spirit in Acts 7:59 as an example for all believers to imitate. Wesley says, "Such a

---

24. Wesley, *Explanatory Notes*, 140.
25. Wesley, *Explanatory Notes*, 670.
26. Wesley, *Explanatory Notes*, 679.
27. Wesley, *Explanatory Notes*, 580–81.

solemn prayer to Christ, in which a departing soul is thus committed into his hands, is such an act of worship, as no good man could have paid to a mere creature; Stephen here worshipping Christ in the very same manner in which Christ worshipped the Father on the cross."[28]

Furthermore, Wesley understood Paul's instructions to the Corinthians to "call upon the name of our Lord Jesus Christ" as straightforward instructions to pray to Christ. Wesley said that this verse "plainly implies that all Christians pray to Christ, as well as to the Father through him."[29] Likewise, the prayer to "direct our way" in 1 Thess 3:11 is "addressed to Christ, as well as to the Father."[30] He commented on Rom 1:7, "Our trust and prayer fix on God, as he is the Father of Christ; and on Christ, as he presents us to the Father."[31] In a letter, he explains a Trinitarian understanding of the relationship of the Father and the Son and the implications it has for prayer:

> The Father and the Son are not "two beings," but "one." As He is man, the Father is doubtless "greater than the Son"; who as such "can do nothing of Himself," and is no more omniscient than omnipresent. And as man He might well say, "I ascend to my Father and your Father," and pray to His Father and His God. He bids His disciples also to pray to Him, but never forbids their praying to Himself. I take this to be the plain, obvious, easy meaning of our Lord's words, and the only one wherein they are reconcilable with an hundred passages both of the Old and New Testament.[32]

Finally, these Scriptures are not just isolated proof texts that Wesley used to justify prayer to Christ. They point to the underlying truth, which Wesley recognized, that Christ is the goal or purpose of all things. In his sermon "Spiritual Worship," Wesley says of Christ, "Lastly, being the true God he is the End of all things; according to that solemn declaration of the Apostle: (Rom. xi.36:) 'Of him, and through him, and to him, are all things:' *Of him* as the Creator,—*through him*, as the Sustainer and Preserver,—and *to him* as the ultimate End of all."[33] Collins commented on this, "Since Christ is the end or *telos*, Wesley encouraged prayer directly to him."[34]

28. Wesley, *Explanatory Notes*, 296.
29. Wesley, *Explanatory Notes*, 408.
30. Wesley, *Explanatory Notes*, 528.
31. Wesley, *Explanatory Notes*, 361.
32. Wesley to Samuel Sparrow, October 9, 1773, 49.
33. Wesley, "Sermon 77," 429.
34. Collins, *Theology*, 352.

Despite this, Wesley felt there was a danger, or at least an impropriety, in elevating prayer to the Son. In a letter to Thomas Maxfield about the state of his Methodist Society, Wesley reproved them, after complimenting their fervency in prayer, on several finer points of their conduct: "But I dislike several things therein: . . . the praying to the Son of God only, or more than to the Father."[35] As a general rule, then, Wesley held prayer to God the Father as the standard.

On the other hand, his advice to one of his correspondents was less spiritually fastidious: "You need not be at all careful in that matter, whether you apply directly to one Person or the other [of the Godhead], seeing He and the Father are one. Pray just as you are led, without reasoning, in all simplicity. Be a little child hanging on Him that loves you."[36] Wesley held personal prayers to a less exacting standard than public prayers.

Prayer and the Holy Spirit

Whereas Christ is pictured as being at the "right hand of God" and fulfilling his duty as the High Priest in the heavenly temple, the Holy Spirit dwells in the hearts of Christians.[37] There, Wesley recognizes four activities of the Holy Spirit related to prayer in the life of the believer. He prays on behalf of Christians, inspires them to pray, helps them pray the right things, and quickens their prayers.

First, the Holy Spirit prays on behalf of Christians. Wesley comments on Rom 8:27 that the heart is the place "wherein the Spirit dwells and intercedes."[38] In his comment on the previous verse, Wesley takes the phrase "the Spirit maketh intercession for us" as taking place "in our hearts, even as Christ does in heaven."[39] This comparison to Christ draws a parallel to Christ's work as the High Priest: offering his own prayers, and offering the prayers of the saints. In a similar manner, the Spirit himself intercedes on behalf of Christians, but he also inspires and empowers their prayers.

The Spirit inspires Christians to pray. In his comment on 1 Thess 5:19, Wesley says, "Wherever [the Spirit] is, it burns; it flames in holy love, in joy,

---

35. Wesley, *Works* (Jackson) 3:121 (October 29, 1762).
36. Wesley to Miss March, July 1, 1772, 326.
37. Wesley, *Explanatory Notes*, 383.
38. Wesley, *Explanatory Notes*, 383.
39. Wesley, *Explanatory Notes*, 383.

prayer, thanksgiving."[40] The presence of the unquenched Spirit in the hearts of believers reveals itself in (among other things), increased prayer.[41]

The Spirit helps Christians to pray the right things. In his comments on the Spirit's "groanings" in Rom 8:26, Wesley says, "The matter of which is from ourselves; but the Spirit forms them; and they are frequently inexpressible, even by the faithful themselves."[42] Although Wesley did not directly relate this verse to the gift of tongues, it forms the broader theological context in which he understood the Spirit to impart supernatural speaking in and understanding of tongues.[43]

The Spirit quickens Christians' prayers, giving life and power to the prayers they utter. When Jesus spoke of being "in the midst" of "two or three gathered together," Wesley comments, "By my Spirit, to quicken their prayers, guide their counsels, and answer their petitions."[44] When Paul directs the Ephesians to pray "by the Spirit," Wesley explains this as "through the influence of the Holy Spirit."[45]

Wesley also felt justified in praying to the Holy Spirit; indeed, he understood the Lord's Prayer as directed to each person of the Trinity: "It is observable, that though the doxology, as well as the petitions of this prayer, is threefold, and is directed to the Father, Son, and Holy Ghost distinctly, yet is the whole fully applicable both to every person, and to the ever-blessed and undivided trinity."[46] He also prayed by name to the Holy Spirit, although the evidence is in song. His official hymnal for Methodism, *A Collection of Hymns for the Use of the People Called Methodists*, has several prayers to and invocations of the Holy Spirit. Hymn 159 begins, "Come, holy, celestial Dove," and ends with, "Come, heavenly Comforter, come."[47] Hymns 341 and 363 invoke the Holy Spirit in both their opening and closing stanzas: "Come, Holy Ghost, all-quick'ning fire."[48] The fourth stanza of 365 begins, "Come,

---

40. Wesley, *Explanatory Notes*, 531.
41. See the section on "Prayer and Sanctification" in chapter 2, "Prayer and Salvation."
42. Wesley, *Explanatory Notes*, 383.
43. See the section on "Praying in Tongues" in chapter 9, "Prayer and Supernatural Manifestations."
44. Wesley, *Explanatory Notes*, 63.
45. Wesley, *Explanatory Notes*, 503.
46. Wesley, *Explanatory Notes*, 26.
47. Wesley, "Hymn 159," 279–80.
48. Wesley, "Hymn 341," 502–3; and "Hymn 363," 532–33.

Holy Ghost, my heart inspire!"[49] Finally, Hymn 516 begins, "Come, thou all-inspiring Spirit."[50] These invitations to the Spirit are direct requests for supernatural presence, and clearly constitute prayers.

Although Wesley did not explain his reasoning in praying to the Holy Spirit, nor cite scriptural support for the practice, it seems likely that for him, given prayer to the Father and the Son, one could not deny prayer to the Holy Spirit while remaining a true Trinitarian. As Thomas Oden put it, "The Holy Ghost is truly God. When we pray to the Spirit, we pray to God."[51] Conversely, if prayer is due to every member of the Godhead, it is also reserved for the members of the Godhead.

Prayer to Others

In Rev 19:10, the apostle John falls at the feet of the angel. Wesley comments that apparently John was "mistaking him for the angel of the covenant," (i.e., God himself). When the angel forbids John to worship him, Wesley concludes, "To pray to or worship the highest creature is flat idolatry."[52] There is no room for giving the creature that which is due solely to the Creator.

Nor did Wesley subscribe to the veneration of the Virgin Mary. However, some things he wrote might call this into question. For instance, in his letter to a Roman Catholic, Wesley writes that he believed that Christ was "born of the blessed Virgin Mary, who, as well after as before she brought him forth, continued a pure and unspotted virgin."[53] Although this belief in the perpetual virginity of Mary was in line with the teachings of his own Anglican Church, it might seem shockingly out of place for such an otherwise-conservative Protestant. Nevertheless, he firmly drew the line when it came to veneration. In commenting on the angel Gabriel's annunciation to Mary, he said, "This salutation gives no room for any pretence of paying adoration to the virgin; as having no appearance of a prayer, or of worship offered to her."[54] Wesley may have been high church, but he was still a Protestant.

49. Wesley, "Hymn 365," 535.
50. Wesley, "Hymn 516," 708.
51. Oden, *Scriptural Christianity*, 226.
52. Wesley, *Explanatory Notes*, 720.
53. Wesley to a Roman Catholic, 81.
54. Wesley, *Explanatory Notes*, 142.

Finally, Wesley denied that Christians should pray to the saints in heaven. He considers the case in his comments on Dives's plea from Hades: "Father Abraham, have mercy on me."[55] In a fairly humorous comment for a book as serious as his *Notes on the New Testament*, he admits, "It cannot be denied, but here is one precedent in Scripture of praying to departed saints: but who is it that prays, and with what success? Will any, who considers this, be fond of copying after him?"[56] In conclusion, Wesley says that 1 Tim 2:5 "excludes all other mediators, as saints and angels, whom the papists set up, and idolatrously worship as such; just as the heathens of old set up many mediators, to pacify their superior gods."[57] Wesley understood prayer to any being outside the Godhead to be strictly forbidden.

Conclusion

Wesley understood prayer to lead to the knowledge of God, and the knowledge of God to lead to prayer in a mutually reinforcing cycle. While Wesley held to the impassibility of God, as classically understood, he also held that prayer is God's ordained means by which to receive his grace. He navigated between these seemingly contradictory statements and taught that prayer changes the situation by changing the readiness of the Christian to receive God's answer to prayer.

The Trinitarian dynamics of prayer affect all who pray, whether they understand them or not. Wesley prayed both to Christ and to the Holy Spirit and saw in their respective prayer ministries insights for Christian prayer. Christ's roles as Prophet, Priest, and King help Christians understand more deeply his role in prayer. As the Prophet, Christ instructs Christians to pray in the very words of God. As Priest, Christ offers his own prayers for Christians and offers their prayers to the Father as well. As King, Christ embodies the ultimate Sovereign and receives prayer from Christians. The Holy Spirit likewise prays for Christians, and also inspires prayer in them and helps them pray the right things. Prayer is an aspect of relationship, and the relational dynamics of prayer with a Trinitarian God form the ground of the Christian life.

---

55. Wesley, *Explanatory Notes*, 186–87.
56. Wesley, *Explanatory Notes*, 186–87.
57. Wesley, *Explanatory Notes*, 540.

— 4 —

Prayer and the Means of Grace

THIS CHAPTER EXPLORES HOW John Wesley understood prayer as a means of grace, indeed, the chief of them, and frequently mentioned prayer in conjunction with reading and fasting. Next, the chapter looks at how, through the means of grace and prayer especially, the religious affections of a believer are stirred and developed, leading to a life characterized by love and holiness.

Definition and Types of Prayer

Wesley defines prayer as "any kind of offering up our desires to God."[1] Recognizing, perhaps, that his definition was a little bald and mechanistic for something so supernatural and central to both the religious affections and sanctification, he then elaborates that "true prayer is the vehemency of holy zeal, the ardour of divine love, arising from a calm, undisturbed soul, moved upon by the Spirit of God."[2] As befitting such a core spiritual activity, prayer is reflective of the Christian's relationship with God. "Prayer may be said to be the breath of our spiritual life. He that lives cannot possibly cease breathing. So much as we really enjoy of the presence of God, so

---

1. Wesley, *Explanatory Notes*, 540.
2. Wesley, *Explanatory Notes*, 540.

much prayer and praise do we offer up without ceasing; else our rejoicing is but delusion."³ A healthy spiritual life, then, is suffused with prayer.

Although Wesley could define prayer briefly and broadly as any kind of offering up our desires to God, when speaking more precisely, he would call this type of prayer "petitioning." Drawing from the anonymous author of the *Whole Duty of Man*,⁴ Wesley identifies the "four grand parts of public prayer" as "deprecation, petition, intercession, and thanksgiving."⁵ Deprecation is defined in the *Whole Duty of Man* as praying "to God to turn away some evil from us. Now the evil may be either the evil of sin, or the evil of punishment."⁶ Petition is making requests of God, intercession is petitioning on behalf of others, and thanksgiving is expressing gratefulness to God. To these four Wesley also added two related disciplines: watching and exercising the presence of God. He considered watching to be a spiritual attentiveness to God and the things of God and a guarding against sin, and understood exercising the presence of God to be a similar spiritual attentiveness to God himself.

As should be clear from his definition of prayer as offering up our desires to God, Wesley considers petition to be the central aspect of prayer: "Whatever other ends are answered by prayer, this is one, and it seems the primary one, that we may have the petitions which we ask of Him. Asking is the appointed means of receiving."⁷ Petitions have two overlapping subcategories: supplication and intercession. Especially vehement petitions are supplications. Wesley describes supplication as "the enlarging upon and pressing our petition."⁸ Elsewhere he defines it as "repeating and urging our prayer, as Christ did in the garden."⁹ When commenting on Paul's instructions to Timothy, Wesley identifies supplication as "here the imploring help in time of need."¹⁰

Wesley writes, "Intercession is prayer for others."¹¹ Wesley understands Paul's command to engage in "supplication for all the saints" as

3. Wesley, *Explanatory Notes*, 531.
4. Johnson, "Liturgical Theology," 70–71.
5. Wesley, *Minutes of Conferences*, 59.
6. Wesley, "Extract from *Whole Duty*," chap 4, part 1, §5.
7. Wesley to Mary Bishop, December 26, 1776, 245.
8. Wesley, *Explanatory Notes*, 513.
9. Wesley, *Explanatory Notes*, 503.
10. Wesley, *Explanatory Notes*, 540.
11. Wesley, *Explanatory Notes*, 540.

meaning "wrestling in fervent, continued intercession for others, especially for the faithful, that they may do all the will of God, and be steadfast to the end."[12] Intercession thrusts the believer out of the comfort of a potentially self-centered prayer life and into concern for others. Intercession makes perfect sense in the logic of relationship. Because relationships exist not just between two isolated individuals, but also as part of a larger web of interpersonal social interconnections, prayer on behalf of others is both reasonable and intuitive: "Reason teaches us to argue from analogy. If *you* (because you have a regard for me) would do more for a third person at my request than otherwise you would have done, how much more will God at the request of His beloved children give blessings to those they pray for which otherwise He would not have given!"[13] Intercession is a natural outgrowth of relationship.

Intercession is not only logical, but scriptural. Wesley comments on God's direction to Job's friends in Job 42:8 to have Job pray for them: "It was not a temporal blessing which was here in question, but a spiritual, the forgiveness of their sin. So when St. Paul said, 'Brethren, pray for us,' he did not desire this on a temporal account only, that 'he might be delivered out of the mouth of the lion,' but on a spiritual, 'that he might speak boldly as he ought to speak.' But the instances of this are innumerable."[14] Even if the instances were innumerable, Wesley still felt the need to furnish his correspondent with another example, and cites Jas 5:14–15: "Let them pray over him; and the prayer of faith shall save the sick; and if he hath committed sins, they shall be forgiven him."[15] Wesley especially highlighted the importance of intercession in relation to general answers to prayer with an additional comment on Eph 6:8, "Perhaps we receive few answers to prayer, because we do not intercede enough for others."[16] He suggested here that the habitual self-centeredness of believers' prayers can make the answers to their prayers an obstacle to their own spiritual growth. In his mercy, perhaps God refuses to answer those prayers until those who pray reach a greater spiritual maturity, indicated by a balance tilted toward concern for others, manifested in intercession for them.

---

12. Wesley, *Explanatory Notes*, 503.
13. Wesley to Mary Bishop, December 26, 1776, 245.
14. Wesley to Mary Bishop, December 26, 1776, 245.
15. Wesley to Mary Bishop, December 26, 1776, 245.
16. Wesley, *Explanatory Notes*, 503.

The third element in Wesley's conception of prayer is thanksgiving. Thanksgiving expresses an acceptance of reality beyond mere resignation (although it includes resignation); in faith, it sees God's hand in all things. Nor is it an optional part of prayer; Wesley writes, "Thanksgiving is inseparable from true prayer: it is almost essentially connected with it. He that always prays is ever giving praise, whether in ease or pain, both for prosperity and for the greatest adversity. He blesses God for all things, looks on them as coming from him, and receives them only for his sake; not choosing nor refusing, liking nor disliking, anything, but only as it is agreeable or disagreeable to his perfect will."[17] This results in both grace and peace in the life of the one giving thanks. "For thanksgiving invites more [grace]: abundant grace."[18] Thanksgiving becomes the "surest mark of a soul free from care, and of prayer joined with true resignation. This is always followed by peace. Peace and thanksgiving are both coupled together, Col 3:15."[19] Thanksgiving is also closely related to praise.

Wesley did not clearly distinguish between thanksgiving and praise (or rejoicing). For instance, he interpreted Jesus's giving thanks for the bread in Matt 15:36 as "he praised God for it, and prayed for a blessing upon it."[20] Insofar as Wesley did distinguish between them, he saw thanksgiving as the result of prayer and rejoicing. In a comment on 1 Thess 5:16, "Rejoice evermore, pray without ceasing, in everything give thanks," he wrote that thanksgiving "is the fruit of both of the former."[21] Thanksgiving and praise might be distinguished, but not easily separated.

Watching is defined by Wesley as "an earnest, constant, persevering exercise. The scripture watching, or waiting, implies steadfast faith, patient hope, labouring love, unceasing prayer; yea, the mighty exertion of all the affections of the soul that a man is capable of."[22] Elsewhere, he defines it as "inwardly attending on God, to know his will, to gain power to do it, and to attain to the blessings we desire."[23] He also charges his preachers to "watch against the world, the devil, ourselves, [and our] besetting sin."[24] In

---

17. Wesley, *Explanatory Notes*, 531.
18. Wesley, *Explanatory Notes*, 455.
19. Wesley, *Explanatory Notes*, 513.
20. Wesley, *Explanatory Notes*, 55.
21. Wesley, *Explanatory Notes*, 531.
22. Wesley, *Explanatory Notes*, 554.
23. Wesley, *Explanatory Notes*, 503.
24. Wesley, *Minutes of Conferences*, 554 ("Large" *Minutes*, 1763).

a comment on 1 John 5:18, Wesley interprets the line, "He that is begotten of God keepeth himself" as meaning that the Christian is always "watching unto prayer."[25] Since the next line of the verse reads that the "wicked one toucheth him not," Wesley saw that spiritual preparedness was the result of watching, defending the Christian against Satan and temptation.

Watching is both a spiritual and a physical discipline. In a comment on 1 Pet 4:7, "Be ye therefore sober, and watch unto prayer," Wesley writes, "Temperance helps watchfulness, and both of them help prayer. Watch, that ye may pray; and pray, that ye may watch."[26] Exercising the presence of God is closely related to watching.

Wesley charges his preachers to exercise the presence of God by asking them, "Do you endeavour to set God always before you? To see his eye continually fixed upon you?"[27] The activity commended in these questions clearly overlaps with the part of watching that he calls "inwardly attending on God."[28] In his study on the means of grace in Wesley's theology, *The Presence of God in the Christian Life*, Henry H. Knight III describes the relationship between watching and exercising the presence of God: "Watching and the exercise of the presence of God are thus mutually reinforcing. Watching helps faith continue and grow through avoiding that which blocks or distorts the vision of faith; exercising the presence of God informs faith of those remaining sins and temptations which need to be removed."[29] Knight saw these two disciplines as the opposite side of self-denial and the taking up of one's cross, insofar as self-denial and taking up one's cross are means of doing good, while watching and exercising the presence of God are means of avoiding evil and harmful activities.[30]

Wesley strongly encouraged the use of all of these and other, more minor types of prayer. He writes that one should pray

> with all sort of prayer, public, private, mental, vocal. Some are careful in respect of one kind of prayer, and negligent in others. If we would have the petitions we ask, let us use all. Some there are who use only mental prayer or ejaculations, and think they are in a state of grace, and use a way of worship, far superior to any other:

25. Wesley, *Explanatory Notes*, 641.
26. Wesley, *Explanatory Notes*, 616.
27. Wesley, *Minutes of Conferences*, 556 ("Large" Minutes, 1763).
28. Wesley, *Explanatory Notes*, 503.
29. Knight, *Presence of God*, 123.
30. Knight, *Presence of God*, 122.

but such only fancy themselves to be above what is really above them; it requiring far more grace to be enabled to pour out a fervent and continued prayer, than to offer up mental aspirations.[31]

However one chooses to pray, one's object, Wesley says, should be the same: "See that it be thy one design to commune with God, to lift up thy heart to him, to pour out thy soul before him."[32] This, whatever the type of prayer, is its soul and essence as Wesley understood it.

Prayer as a Means of Grace

The importance of prayer is tied to its function as one of the means of grace. Wesley defines the "means of grace" as "outward signs, words, or actions, ordained of God, and appointed for this end, to be the ordinary channels whereby he might convey to men, preventing, justifying, or sanctifying grace."[33] Wesley was forceful in establishing that the means of grace had no virtue in and of themselves. Three times in his sermon "The Means of Grace," he felt the need to emphasize this truth. First, he says, "We allow, likewise, that all outward means whatever, if separate from the Spirit of God, cannot profit at all, cannot conduce, in any degree, either to the knowledge or love of God."[34] Later, he says, "We know that there is no inherent power in the words that are spoken in prayer, in the letter of Scripture read, the sound thereof heard . . . but that it is God alone who is the Giver of every good gift, the Author of all grace; that the whole power is of Him, whereby, through any of these, there is any blessing conveyed to our souls."[35] Finally, he revisits prayer as a means of grace when he addresses the question of whether Christ is the only means of grace: "Every believer in Christ is deeply convinced that there is no merit but in Him; that there is no merit in any of his own works; not in uttering the prayer, or searching the Scripture . . . so that if no more be intended by the expression some have used, 'Christ is the only means of grace,' than

---

31. Wesley, *Explanatory Notes*, 503.
32. Wesley, "Sermon 26," 330.
33. Wesley, "Sermon 16," 187.
34. Wesley, "Sermon 16," 188.
35. Wesley, "Sermon 16," 188.

this,—that He is the only meritorious cause of it, it cannot be gainsayed by any who know the grace of God."[36]

Knight argues that, for Wesley, grace is relational.[37] This implies that grace is not tied solely to some single past or future event. Although the past and future salvific activity of God is important, "salvation is a present experience, a new way of life which is lived in an ongoing relationship with the living God."[38] The act of bestowing grace is God's "triune act of love,"[39] and "all means of grace have as their end the life of love."[40] Knight asserted that, in Wesley's theology, since grace is not merely a commodity to be divinely bestowed, but that since the Christian life is essentially a relationship with God, then "grace is not only the means to that life, but the Christian life is itself *essentially graced*."[41] Thus, any attempt to separate out grace and place it "objectively" in some means (whether internal or external), is doomed to failure. "Grace is relational and personal, not mechanistic and institutional."[42] The believer's relationship with God is both the source of grace and its primary destination.

Prayer is the foremost of all the means of grace. Wesley says that "the chief of these means are prayer, whether in secret or with the great congregation"[43] and shortly after that adds, "And, First, all who desire the grace of God are to wait for it in the way of prayer."[44] Selleck points out that "prayer heads all his [Wesley's] lists of the instituted means of grace."[45] Wesley even went so far as to say, "Prayer is certainly the grand means of drawing near to God; and all others are helpful to us only so far as they are mixed with or prepare us for this."[46] It should come as no surprise, then, that Wesley sees inward spiritual darkness happening when one neglects private prayer: "The want whereof cannot be supplied by any other ordinance whatever. Nothing can be more plain, than that the life of God in the

---

36. Wesley, "Sermon 16," 189.
37. Knight, *Presence of God*, 8.
38. Knight, *Presence of God*, 9.
39. Knight, *Presence of God*, 9.
40. Knight, *Presence of God*, 4.
41. Knight, *Presence of God*, 10.
42. Knight, *Presence of God*, 30.
43. Wesley, "Sermon 16," 188.
44. Wesley, "Sermon 16," 190.
45. Selleck, "Common Prayer," 99.
46. Wesley to Miss March, March 29, 1760, 90.

soul does not continue, much less increase, unless we use all opportunities of communion with God, and pouring out our hearts before him."[47] Wesley encouraged a full panoply of content in prayer, advising, "Consider both your outward and inward state, and vary your prayers accordingly."[48] Knight comments on this: "Christian prayer necessarily includes this full range of elements because the relationship with God is itself multidimensional."[49] Prayer encompasses the fullness of one's relationship with God.

Prayer is not only an indirect means to God's sanctifying grace—that is, through normal daily relating to God through prayer—but also a direct means through the simple expedient of asking. Wesley says, "There is yet another remedy left, and one that is frequently found effectual, when no other method avails; this is prayer. Therefore whatever you desire or want, either for others or for your own soul, 'Ask, and it shall be given you; seek, and ye shall find; knock, and it shall be opened unto you.' The neglect of this is a . . . grand hindrance of holiness."[50] Knight comments on this passage, "The failure to ask for increased holiness in prayer is one reason persons fail to grow in the Christian life."[51] Holiness is there for the asking, and Wesley expects God to give it.

Knight sees the means of grace in Wesley's theology operating in a cycle with faith in the Christian life: "Convincing, justifying, and sanctifying grace all share with prevenient grace the common pattern of God taking the initiative, and the human responding to that initiative. . . . Thus grace enables and invites a faithful response; faith in turn is open to God and desires a relationship with God."[52] At every step of their relationship, God initiates and humans respond. God initiates with *grace*, and humans respond with *faith*. This is true of the entirety of the relationship believers have with God, from the beginning in prevenient grace to its culmination in sanctification and beyond. But grace and faith are not exclusive of love. This cycle works in concert with the receiving of God's love and the Christian's response in love: "Wesley saw prayer as the integration of activity and receptiveness. Because we seek God and ask for promised gifts of grace, we become increasingly aware of God's presence and open

47. Wesley, "Sermon 46," 81.
48. Wesley, "Sermon 89," 30.
49. Knight, *Presence of God*, 119.
50. Wesley, "Sermon 30," 401.
51. Knight, *Presence of God*, 118.
52. Knight, *Presence of God*, 170.

to God's transformation of our lives. And as we respond in love, our relationship with God grows."[53] An initiation of grace is an initiation in love. A response in faith is a response in love. Prayer is the locus of both this divine activity and the human response. The exchange of grace and faith is not an economic exchange, but a relational one; neither grace nor faith is a commodity, but an act of love. Knight explains, "A true desire for God is not a desire to 'get' grace, as if God could be possessed; rather it is a desire to know God and to live in response to God's love. It is a giving of ourselves to God, in response to God's self-giving love. . . . Faith, then, involves active receptivity and response; it seeks through the means of grace the God who has already sought us in love."[54]

Prayer and the Religious Affections

The love of God, then, is the foundation for holiness, and the revelation of the love of God through the Spirit by the means of grace is what enables the believer to love him. Wesley understood sanctification, the spiritual formation of the Christian character, as being in some sense the growth of this love. In the language of the time, it was the increase of the "religious affections"—the inflammation of zeal, longing, and loving desire for God (and, as a necessary consequence, of love for one's fellow men and women). Wesley writes, "Prayer is any kind of offering up our desires to God. But true prayer is the vehemency of holy zeal, the ardour of divine love, arising from a calm, undisturbed soul, moved upon by the Spirit of God."[55] However, one must remember that in Wesley's theology, "our love . . . is not a possession apart from God but a temper or affection which is intrinsically relational."[56] The Spirit reveals God's love, which strengthens the relationship of the believer in affection toward God.

The same Spirit that reveals the love of God also initiates prayer through both conviction of the truth and the love of God and humans. Prayer, however, is not just requesting the fulfillment of desires, but is also the development of the Godward desires of the believer for conformity to the image of God. That is, desire for God is itself a mark of holiness. Wesley writes, "Indeed all the words in the world are not equivalent to one holy

---

53. Knight, *Presence of God*, 118.
54. Knight, *Presence of God*, 170.
55. Wesley, *Explanatory Notes*, 540.
56. Knight, *Presence of God*, 10.

desire. And the very best prayers are but vain repetitions, if they are not the language of the heart."[57] Of the Lord's Prayer Wesley writes, "This prayer uttered from the heart, and in its true and full meaning, is indeed the badge of a real Christian: for is not he such whose first and most ardent desire is the glory of God."[58] To that end, prayer is a spiritual discipline. "The chief thing wanting is, a fit disposition on our part to receive his grace and blessing. Consequently, one great office of prayer is, to produce such a disposition in us: to exercise our dependence on God; to increase our desire of the things we ask for; to make us so sensible of our wants, that we may never cease wrestling till we have prevailed for the blessing."[59] Through prayer, the believer requests the transformation of holiness into the image of God, and through prayer, that transformation is partially worked.

Unsurprisingly, then, the prayers Wesley wrote and published are full of requests for God to transform the heart and inflame the desire of the one who prays: "Let his [the Spirit's] blessed inspiration prevent and assist me in all the duties of this thy sacred day, that . . . my flat and cold desires quickened into fervent longings and thirstings after thee. O let me join in the prayers and praises of thy Church with ardent and heavenly affection [and] . . . give thy strength unto thy servant, that thy love may fill my heart."[60] In praying for others, he writes, "May they once taste and see how gracious thou art . . . that their desires may be always flying up towards thee, that they may render thee love."[61]

God's response to these requests is to draw the believer further along the path of conformity to his image, through the transforming power of his love. Through prayer, the Holy Spirit gives immediate and direct help, pouring out the love of God into the heart of the believer. "Suppose, for instance, you are employed in private prayer, and God pours his love into your heart. God then acts *immediately* on your soul; and the love of him which you then experience, is as *immediately* breathed into you by the Holy Ghost, as if you had lived seventeen hundred years ago."[62]

Besides God's direct response to the request of the believer, prayer itself indirectly increases faith and love. Knight explains that "because prayer is

---

57. Wesley, *Explanatory Notes*, 25.
58. Wesley, *Explanatory Notes*, 169.
59. Wesley, *Explanatory Notes*, 25.
60. Wesley, *Forms of Prayer*, 204.
61. Wesley, *Forms of Prayer*, 208.
62. Wesley, *Farther Appeal, Part I*, 107.

communion with God, it invites a conscious, intentional relationship with God."[63] In praying, the believer encounters God and develops a relationship with him. Knight continues: "The very act of praying itself gives shape to the relationship and the Christian life."[64] Furthermore, "all [prayers] focus the attention of the one who prays upon God, but in ways that nurture different affections: hope, humility, love of neighbor, and gratitude, but in all cases love for the God who promises, forgives, serves, and blesses. In the full range of prayer, presumption is countered with honest confession, complacency with active love, and despair with expectant hope."[65]

This cycle of love is the progress of sanctification. "It is in consequence of our knowing God loves us, that we love him, and love our neighbour as ourselves. . . . Standing fast in this liberty from sin and sorrow, wherewith Christ hath made them free, real Christians 'rejoice evermore, pray without ceasing, and in everything give thanks.'"[66] These three actions—rejoicing evermore, praying without ceasing, and in everything giving thanks—are the hallmarks of a Christian who has been made perfect in holiness, who has attained what Wesley called "Christian perfection."[67]

Prayer and Reading

Wesley considered reading, both the Scriptures and other edifying literature, to be a means of grace, saying, "With regard to you, the great danger is that you should forsake the sacred channels of His grace. Only abide in the way. Read, meditate, pray as you *can*, though not as you *would*. Then God will return and abundantly lift up the light of His countenance upon you."[68] In the same breath that Wesley recommended prayer, he often recommended reading. For instance, he writes to Mrs. Woodhouse, "Continually stir up the gift of God which is in you, not only by continuing to hear His word at all opportunities, but by reading, by meditation, and above

---

63. Knight, *Presence of God*, 117.
64. Knight, *Presence of God*, 117.
65. Knight, *Presence of God*, 119–20.
66. Wesley, "Sermon 114," 269–70.
67. See chapter 12 of this book for an extended discussion of this topic.
68. Wesley to Mrs. Gair, November 5, 1774, 117.

all by private prayer."[69] Similarly, he wrote to Ann Foard, "Let no day pass without more or less private prayer, reading, and meditation."[70]

Many of Wesley's recommendations were for prayerfully reading the Scriptures. One of the "instituted means of grace is searching the Scriptures. Wesley recommended a constant and regular reading of the Bible, done in order (*lectio continua*), both preceded and followed by prayer."[71] These prayers should not be merely perfunctory. Wesley felt that the importance of the Scripture should be matched by the seriousness of one's prayers, especially considering the transformative power of Scripture in one's life. "Serious and earnest prayer should be constantly used before we consult the oracles of God. . . . Our reading should likewise be closed with prayer, that what we read may be written on our hearts."[72] But prayers are not merely spiritual bookends on either side of Scripture reading. Prayerfully reading Scripture involves praying *while* reading, as well. Does one search the Scriptures, Wesley asks, by reading "some part of every day . . . with much prayer preceding, accompanying, and following?"[73] Hopefully, one's practice of reading is part of one's larger habit of prayer.

However, Wesley also clearly recommended prayerfully reading other edifying works besides Scripture. He advises a female correspondent, "Spend some time every day in private prayer, in meditation, and in reading the *Notes on the New Testament*, the first volume of *Sermons*, and the *Appeals*."[74] To a male correspondent, he writes, "Spend the first hour in the morning and from five to six in the evening in private prayer and reading the Scriptures in order, with the *Notes* and any other closely practical book. . . . Spend some time afterwards in the morning in reading Bishop Pearson or any other book of divinity; and spend more or less time in the afternoon in reading history, poetry, or philosophy."[75]

In order to help people find reliable, edifying spiritual books, he abridged and reprinted many works of devotional literature in his *Christian Library*, which eventually ran to thirty volumes. He recommended the *Christian Library* to all his preachers, saying, "What other books

69. Wesley to Mrs. Woodhouse, May 17, 1766, 12.
70. Wesley to Ann Foard, January 15, 1767, 37.
71. Selleck, "Common Prayer," 99.
72. Wesley, Preface to *Explanatory Notes*, 253.
73. Wesley, *Minutes of Conferences*, 550 ("Large" *Minutes*, 1763).
74. Wesley to Ann Foard, August 21, 1766, 25.
75. Wesley to Alexander Knox, June 5, 1778, 314.

do you read? Is it wise to read any till you have read our tracts, and the Christian Library?"[76] Although he does not mention the *Christian Library* specifically, it was exactly the sort of thing people like John Trembath, one of his itinerant preachers, needed to read. In perhaps his longest explanation of the importance of reading, Wesley ascribes John Trembath's weak preaching to his lack of reading:

> What has exceedingly hurt you in time past, nay, and I fear to this day, is want of reading. I scarce ever knew a preacher read so little. And perhaps by neglecting it you have lost the taste for it. Hence your talent in preaching does not increase. It is just the same as it was seven years ago. It is lively, but not deep; there is little variety; there is no compass of thought. Reading only can supply this, with meditation and daily prayer. You wrong yourself greatly by omitting this. You can never be a deep preacher without it any more than a thorough Christian. Oh begin! Fix some part of every day for private exercises. You may acquire taste which you have not; what is tedious at first will afterwards be pleasant. Whether you like it or no, read and pray daily. It is for your life; there is no other way: else you will be a trifler all your days, and a pretty, superficial preacher.[77]

Prayer and Fasting

Wesley strongly encouraged fasting, both among his ministers and the congregations. He believed that fasting was commanded by Jesus in the Sermon on the Mount: "For the commanding us to do anything *thus*, is an unquestionable command to do that thing."[78] As a means of grace, fasting has been appointed by God,[79] and "blessings are to be obtained in the use of his means, which are no otherwise attainable."[80] Wesley believed so strongly in the importance of fasting that he declares, "The man that never fasts is no more in the way to heaven, than the man that never prays."[81]

---

76. Wesley, *Minutes of Conferences*, 550 ("Large" *Minutes*, 1763).
77. Wesley to John Trembath, August 17, 1760, 103.
78. Wesley, "Sermon 27," 354.
79. Wesley, "Sermon 27," 351, 353.
80. Wesley, "Sermon 27," 353.
81. Wesley, "Sermon 116," 289.

Fasting is not only comparable in importance to prayer, but also clearly empowers and supports it.

Wesley saw fasting as an aid to and intensifier of prayer. He says that believers fast "to add seriousness and earnestness to our prayers."[82] He calls it "an help to prayer," especially "when we set apart larger portions of time for private prayer."[83] That is, as an intensifier of prayer, it intensifies the commitment and dedication of the one who prays, prompting him or her to pray for longer periods, as well as with greater focus and less temptation to distraction. As an aid to prayer, "it has so frequently been found a means, in the hand of God, of confirming and increasing, not one virtue . . . [but] every holy and heavenly affection."[84] The example of godly men in the Bible provided justification to Wesley for this relationship between fasting and prayer; he says, "Thus, we may observe, the men of God, in ancient times, always joined prayer and fasting together,"[85] and "the Apostles always joined fasting with prayer when they desired the blessing of God."[86] Furthermore, his own experience confirmed this, and his journal testifies to the grace that God gives in response to prayer joined with fasting. For example, "*Friday, 10*, we observed as a day of fasting and prayer. It was at our last meeting that we found the answer of our prayers. It seemed as if the windows of heaven were opened; the Spirit of grace and supplication was poured out. Many were filled with consolation; and many who had grown weary resolved to set out anew."[87] On another occasion, Wesley writes, "We observed *Friday, 19*, as a day of fasting and prayer, for a revival of his work. . . . And then it was that God touched the hearts of the people, even of those that were 'twice dead.'"[88] Wesley's experience of fasting was consistently positive.

As a supplement to prayer, Wesley saw two main purposes for fasting. The first was to turn away the wrath of God.[89] His impassioned letter to the Earl of Dartmouth on the difficulties they were having with the American colonies ends with a plea for fasting: "But we Englishmen are too wise to acknowledge that God has anything to do in the world!

---

82. Wesley, "Sermon 27," 358.
83. Wesley, "Sermon 27," 351.
84. Wesley, "Sermon 27," 351.
85. Wesley, "Sermon 27," 360.
86. Wesley, "Sermon 27," 352.
87. Wesley, *Works* (Jackson) 3:287 (July 10, 1767).
88. Wesley, *Works* (Jackson) 3:363 (May 19, 1769).
89. Wesley, "Sermon 27," 351.

Otherwise should we not seek Him by fasting and prayer before He lets the lifted thunder drop? O my Lord, if your Lordship can do anything let it not be wanting! For God's sake, for the sake of the King, of the nation, of your lovely family, remember Rehoboam! Remember Philip the Second! Remember King Charles the First!"[90]

The second purpose for fasting was for "obtaining whatever blessings we stand in need of."[91] These blessings were not limited to "chastity only, (as some have idly imagined, without any ground either from Scripture, reason, or experience,) but also seriousness of spirit, earnestness, sensibility and tenderness of conscience, deadness to the world, and consequently the love of God."[92] Especially impressive to Wesley was the power conferred in casting out demons. When Jesus explains why the disciples could not drive out a demon, "this kind goeth not out but by prayer and fasting," Wesley comments, "What a testimony is here of the efficacy of fasting, when added to fervent prayer! Some kinds of devils the apostles had cast out before this, without fasting."[93] Elsewhere, he used the same passage to highlight the importance of fasting as an appointed means of God, saying, "[prayer and fasting are] the appointed means of attaining that faith whereby the very devils are subject unto you."[94] These two purposes are not the only reasons Wesley gives for fasting, however.

Knight identifies five other reasons for fasting in Wesley's "Sermon on the Mount, VII": "sorrow for sin, bodily health, avoidance of excessive consumption, self-punishment . . . and as an aid to prayer."[95] The last point is especially important, as it is mentioned over and again in Wesley's writings: "When you seek God with fasting added to prayer, you cannot seek His face in vain."[96] "When two or three agree to seek God by fasting and prayer, it cannot be that their labour should be in vain."[97] "God will hearken to the prayer that goeth not out of feigned lips, especially when

---

90. Wesley to the Earl of Dartmouth, June 14, 1775, 159–60.
91. Wesley, "Sermon 27," 352.
92. Wesley, "Sermon 27," 351.
93. Wesley, *Explanatory Notes*, 60.
94. Wesley, "Sermon 27," 353.
95. Knight, *Presence of God*, 120–21.
96. Wesley to George Cussons, November 18, 1768, 112.
97. Wesley to Mrs. Bennis, September 10, 1773, 40.

fasting is joined therewith."[98] Knight analyzes two significant reasons Wesley gives that point to fasting's importance:

> While Wesley does not say why fasting is such an important aid to prayer, two of his reasons for fasting suggest an answer. First, he argues that "sorrow for sin, and a strong apprehension of the wrath of God" are the natural grounds of fasting. Preoccupied with this eternally significant concern, one forgets to eat, abstaining "not only from pleasant, but even needful food." Here fasting is a recognition of oneself as a sinner before God and an expression of the resulting penitential and non-presumptive relationship.
>
> Second, fasting is the avoidance of excessive consumption of food, along with a "carelessness and levity of spirit" and an increase in "foolish and unholy desires, yea, unclean and vile affections" which accompany such consumption. This observation is in accord with the insights of patristic asceticism concerning the connection of eating with a more general rise in sensuality. The danger which fasting helps avoid is a dissipation of desire, and a corresponding turning away from God.[99]

Knight saw a connection that is ultimately relational in the action of fasting, which accounts for its importance in joining with prayer. Through fasting, one apprehends the truth about one's standing before God, and avoids those distractions which would dull one's desire for God.

To prevent this relational value from being nullified, Wesley was concerned with how fasting was performed. His first concern with fasting was that it be done unto the Lord, "with our eye singly fixed on Him,"[100] and not for the praise of men. His second concern was that Christians remember that fasting itself merits nothing, and that it is "only a way which God hath ordained, wherein we wait for his unmerited mercy; and wherein, without any desert of ours, he hath promised freely to give us his blessing."[101] In this way the effectiveness of fasting would be preserved.

---

98. Wesley to Robert Carr Brackenbury, November 24, 1785, 301.
99. Knight, *Presence of God*, 121.
100. Wesley, "Sermon 27," 357.
101. Wesley, "Sermon 27," 358.

Conclusion

Wesley described four major types of prayer, as well as two closely related exercises (watching and exercising the presence of God), all of which are important to the growth of a Christian life. Prayer is a means of grace through which God's grace is appropriated by the believer in the context of a growing spiritual relationship that results in increased holiness and love. Wesley considered prayer especially appropriate to accompany spiritual reading, both Scriptures and other works. Fasting, likewise, is especially appropriate to accompany prayer, as it functions as an aid to intensify prayer. Combined, these ideas formed the thrust of Wesley's teaching on prayer as a means of grace. Having established this theoretical foundation, Wesley took the Lord's Prayer as the best practical guide for how to pray.

— 5 —

The Lord's Prayer

Introduction

As one of the primary means of growth of the Christian life, Christ taught his disciples to pray what is now known as the Lord's Prayer, recorded in slightly different forms in both Matthew and Luke. In his sermon, "Sermon on the Mount, VI," John Wesley analyzed this prayer (Matt 6:1–15). Wesley writes that he considered the Lord's Prayer to be "a most perfect and universal form of prayer,"[1] in fact, "the model and standard of all our prayers,"[2] thus establishing what he considered normative practice for Christian prayer. Moreover, he says, it "contains all our duty to God and man," including "what we must first know of God, before we can pray."[3] It therefore also reveals the theological underpinnings necessary to justify and establish that normative practice.

Wesley called the Lord's Prayer the "divine form"[4] of prayer, and understood Christ to command the use of the very words of the prayer in his opening words of the Lukan form of the prayer: "When ye pray, say . . ."[5] This is certainly not to be understood as *confining* Christian

1. Wesley, *Explanatory Notes*, 25.
2. Wesley, "Sermon 26," 332.
3. Wesley, "Sermon 26," 333.
4. Wesley, "Sermon 26," 332.
5. Wesley, *Explanatory Notes*, 169.

prayer to repeating these words; Wesley himself wrote several books of model prayers (*A Collection of Forms of Prayer for every Day in the Week*, *A Collection of Prayers for Families*, and *Prayers for Children*). However, he also clearly approved of the use of the Lord's Prayer among believers as an aid to training them how to pray for themselves.

Wesley broke down the Lord's Prayer into a three-part structure, consisting of the preface, the petitions, and the doxology. This chapter examines each part of the structure, analyzing Wesley's understanding of it.

The Lord's Prayer: Preface

The first part of the Lord's Prayer, the preface, "lays a general foundation for prayer"[6] two different ways: first, in communicating the basics of theology, and second, in the attitudes "which are most essentially requisite, if we desire either our prayers or our lives should find acceptance with [God]."[7] The preface consists of the single line, "Our Father, which art in heaven."

In the word *Father*, Wesley found a wealth of theological implications. *Father* communicated to him both the essential goodness of God and the expression of that goodness in love toward his children.[8] This love and goodness includes God's willingness to bless, which is the foundation for petition in this prayer and all others. Furthermore, *Father* points toward God's relationship to humans as their Creator. As the ultimate source of every creature's existence, God has given the gift of life. Since every person's relationship with God was formed out of this gift of life, Wesley urges, "Let us ask, and he will not withhold any good thing from the work of his own hands."[9] However, God has given each creature more than just a one-time gift of life.

God is not only the ultimate source of every creature's existence, but as Father, he is also the Preserver, and thus the immediate source of every creature's continued existence. In light of this, Wesley again urges, "So much the more boldly let us come to him."[10] If each successive breath is a gift of God, then surely one's continued life speaks to God's continued willingness to accept those who come to him.

6. Wesley, "Sermon 26," 333.
7. Wesley, "Sermon 26," 333.
8. Wesley, "Sermon 26," 333.
9. Wesley, "Sermon 26," 333.
10. Wesley, "Sermon 26," 333.

Finally and most importantly, God is "the Father of our Lord Jesus Christ, and of all that believe in him."[11] Wesley followed this declaration with a sampling of the benefits those who believe in Christ have already received: redemption, cleansing from sin, health, adoption, the Holy Spirit, and new life. Wesley finishes this section with this summary: "We pray, because we love; and 'we love him, because he first loved us.'"[12]

In the word *Our*, Wesley likewise found a wealth of theological implications. In conjunction with the following term *Father*, Wesley established God as the Father of all. God is "*ours* in the most extensive sense,"[13] he writes. This includes not only all men, but angels as well, the entire universe, and all "both in heaven and earth."[14]

If God is truly the Father of all, Wesley reasoned, then it must follow that God loves all. He is no respecter of persons; God created all and loves all that he created. God especially loves those who have trusted in Jesus Christ for salvation, but this should not instill in the believer a sense of superiority. Rather, Wesley said, in light of the sacrifice of Christ, believers are all the more obligated to love others. As Christ's sacrifice was because "God so loved the world," so should believers also love the world in imitation of their Father.

The final part of the preface to the Lord's Prayer is the phrase "which art in heaven." Although Scripture speaks of heaven being inhabited by a multitude of angels, in reference to the Father this phrase speaks of his divine attributes. According to Wesley, it indicates his attributes of omniscience, sovereignty, omnipotence, and omnipresence.

First, from heaven, the Father beholds "all things, both in heaven and earth; knowing every creature, and all the works of every creature, and every possible event from everlasting to everlasting: the almighty Lord and Ruler of all, superintending and disposing all things."[15] His eye "pervades the whole sphere of created being,"[16] such that all men and angels "cry out with wonder and amazement"[17] at the depth of his knowledge and wisdom. Second, being enthroned in heaven speaks of his sovereign position

11. Wesley, "Sermon 26," 333.
12. Wesley, "Sermon 26," 333.
13. Wesley, "Sermon 26," 333.
14. Wesley, "Sermon 26," 334.
15. Wesley, *Explanatory Notes*, 25.
16. Wesley, "Sermon 26," 334.
17. Wesley, "Sermon 26," 334.

as "King of kings and Lord of lords, the blessed and only Potentate."[18] Third, it speaks of his omnipotence, as he is "strong and girded about with power, doing whatsoever pleaseth"[19] him. Finally, although heaven is the Father's throne, he "fillest heaven and earth, the whole expanse of space"[20] in his omnipresence.

The theological implications Wesley derived from the six-word preface of the Lord's Prayer are extensive. Nevertheless, as constituting "what we must know of God, before we can pray in confidence of being heard,"[21] these implications are generally consistent with what he has written elsewhere about the prayers of unbelievers.[22] For instance, Wesley says of Cornelius in Acts 10 that "every one who seeks faith in Christ, should seek it in prayer"[23] whether the individual is a believer yet or not. Wesley held that to pray, one must certainly have a clear understanding of both God's transcendent nature and role as Creator of all that exists.

The Lord's Prayer: Petitions

In training believers how to pray, Wesley saw the Lord's Prayer as encompassing all possible acceptable prayers, which he expressed in three ways. First, he says, it contains "all we can reasonably or innocently pray for."[24] Second, it contains "all we can reasonably or innocently desire."[25] Third, it contains, "all our duty to God and man; whatsoever things are pure and holy, . . . whatsoever is acceptable in his sight, whatsoever it is whereby we may profit our neighbour, being expressed or implied therein."[26] Anything one might wish to request that does not fit within the petitions of the Lord's Prayer is, therefore, unfit "to have a place in our desires."[27]

This second section of the Lord's Prayer begins with the first petition, "Hallowed be thy name." Wesley writes, "The name of God is God himself;

18. Wesley, "Sermon 26," 334.
19. Wesley, "Sermon 26," 334.
20. Wesley, "Sermon 26," 334.
21. Wesley, "Sermon 26," 333.
22. See "Prayers of Unbelievers," in chapter 2 of this book.
23. Wesley, *Explanatory Notes*, 302.
24. Wesley, "Sermon 26," 332.
25. Wesley, "Sermon 26," 332.
26. Wesley, "Sermon 26," 333.
27. Wesley, "Sermon 26," 332.

the nature of God, so far as it can be discovered to man."[28] This builds on the truths contained in the preface, and includes his existence, "all his attributes or perfections,"[29] and his eternity. It also includes "His Trinity in Unity, and Unity in Trinity; . . . His essential purity and holiness;—and above all, his love."[30] To pray for God's name to be hallowed, one prays, first, for his name—and by extension, his person, nature, and attributes—to be known "by all intelligent beings,"[31] and second, that his name would be "duly honoured, and feared, and loved"[32] by all.

The second petition is "Thy kingdom come." This is the foundation and prerequisite to the first petition. For God's name, as encompassing his nature and character, to be truly known by all intelligent beings, God's Kingdom must first come. God's Kingdom comes in two main ways: individually, person by person, as each one repents and believes, and corporately and suddenly on the day of Christ's return. Additionally, it also includes the prayer for the coming of the "everlasting kingdom, the kingdom of glory in heaven."[33]

When an individual repents and believes, then the kingdom of God is "set up in the believer's heart."[34] The evidence that "'the Lord God Omnipotent' then 'reigneth'"[35] is that the believer "goeth on in the soul conquering and to conquer, till he hath put all things under his feet, till 'every thought is brought into captivity to the obedience of Christ.'"[36]

As Christians share the gospel from person to person, they also look for the day of Christ's return. Moreover, believers pray for the hastening of his return, and this is the substance of the petition, "Thy kingdom come." It is appropriate for believers to pray for this, as it is the fulfillment of their desire for humankind to be "filled with righteousness, and peace, and joy"[37] until the coming of his everlasting heavenly kingdom. This everlasting heavenly

---

28. Wesley, "Sermon 26," 334.
29. Wesley, "Sermon 26," 335.
30. Wesley, "Sermon 26," 335.
31. Wesley, "Sermon 26," 335.
32. Wesley, "Sermon 26," 335.
33. Wesley, "Sermon 26," 336.
34. Wesley, "Sermon 26," 335.
35. Wesley, "Sermon 26," 335.
36. Wesley, "Sermon 26," 335–36.
37. Wesley, "Sermon 26," 336.

kingdom is "the continuation and perfection of the kingdom of grace on earth,"[38] and is also part of the petition, "Thy kingdom come."

Wesley extrapolates this petition in his *Explanatory Notes on the New Testament*: "May thy kingdom of grace come quickly, and swallow up all the kingdoms of the earth: may all mankind, receiving thee, O Christ, for their king, truly believing in thy name, be filled with righteousness, and peace, and joy; with holiness and happiness, till they are removed hence into thy kingdom of glory, to reign with thee for ever and ever."[39] Praying for the kingdom of God is praying for the fullness of righteousness to reign over the earth.

The third petition of the Lord's Prayer is "Thy will be done on earth, as it is in heaven." This petition is built on the second petition, as it is "the necessary and immediate consequence wherever the kingdom of God is come."[40] Wesley understood that this petition is not primarily a prayer for an attitude of resignation concerning the will of God, but rather, it is a prayer for "an active, conformity to the will of God."[41] This was an important distinction for Wesley, because resignation in prayer was closely tied to Quietism, which Wesley ultimately rejected in his theology.

"As it is in heaven" indicates that the heavenly practice is the pattern which Christians are praying will be established completely on earth. Wesley identified several key features of how God's will is done by the angels in heaven. First, God's will is done willingly. Angels do not obey primarily out of a sense of duty; rather, obedience "is their highest glory and joy."[42] Second, they do God's will continually, without interruption or cessation.[43] Third, they do God's will perfectly, for "no defect belongs to angelic minds."[44] Finally, they do God's will completely, in that there is no part of what God wills for them that they do not carry out.[45]

Wesley then applied this heavenly pattern to the petition for God's will to be done on earth. When Christians pray "Thy will be done on earth, as it is in heaven," they are praying for each of these things as they

38. Wesley, "Sermon 26," 336.
39. Wesley, *Explanatory Notes*, 25.
40. Wesley, "Sermon 26," 336.
41. Wesley, "Sermon 26," 337.
42. Wesley, "Sermon 26," 337.
43. Wesley, "Sermon 26," 337.
44. Wesley, "Sermon 26," 337.
45. Wesley, "Sermon 26," 337.

apply to humanity. That is, that humanity would do God's will willingly, continually, perfectly—as Scripture promised to "make them perfect in every good work to do his will"[46]—and completely; that humanity would "do the whole will of God as he willeth, in the manner that pleases him . . . and *because* it is his will."[47] All of these requests are entailed in the third petition of the Lord's Prayer.

The fourth petition of the Lord's Prayer is "Give us this day our daily bread." While the first three petitions have focused on corporate needs, in this petition, the focus shifts from humanity as a whole to the individual and his or her needs. The construction still allows for a corporate application, however.

"Bread" is understood by Wesley to refer to "all things needful."[48] Not only physical bread but spiritual nourishment is implied in the term. Wesley pointed out that many of the early church fathers also understood it to mean the "sacramental bread,"[49] but did not push this meaning himself. Understanding "bread" as both physical and spiritual nourishment implies the entire complex web of human needs, and so supports petition regarding anything that weighs on the mind or precipitates worry. However, this is tempered with the term "daily," which necessarily limits the scope of potential topics to a manageable portion.

Wesley interpreted the term "daily" in a simple sense, that one's prayers should focus on "what is sufficient for this day."[50] This is reiterated in the phrase "give us this day." Wesley explains that this is so "we might look on every day as a fresh gift of God, another life, which we may devote to his glory; and that every evening may be as the close of life, beyond which we are to see nothing but eternity."[51] Rather than forbidding petitions about longer-term issues, then, "daily" and "this day" are formative phrases meant to instill a focus on the present in the one praying.

"Give us" is a plea for mercy from God. Wesley explains, "We ask him to give, what we can no more procure for ourselves, than we can merit it at his hands."[52] This plea in no way undermines or invalidates the importance

---

46. Wesley, "Sermon 26," 337–38.
47. Wesley, "Sermon 26," 338.
48. Wesley, "Sermon 26," 338.
49. Wesley, "Sermon 26," 338.
50. Wesley, "Sermon 26," 338.
51. Wesley, "Sermon 26," 339.
52. Wesley, "Sermon 26," 338.

of human diligence in work, for it is God's will that humans work as if "our success were the natural effect of our own wisdom and strength."[53] On the other hand, even working in their own strength, believers are to "depend on Him" as though "we had done nothing."[54]

"And forgive us our trespasses, as we forgive them that trespass against us" is the fifth petition of the Lord's Prayer. Wesley points out that this petition has a natural relationship with the previous one, "as nothing but sin can hinder the bounty of God."[55] Furthermore, this forgiveness (both the receiving of it from heaven and the giving of it to others) is done "not once, but continually."[56]

Wesley interprets the phrase "our trespasses" in terms of debt, in accordance with how sins are "frequently represented in Scripture."[57] Humans as sinners already owe a debt to God they can never repay, and every sin increases this debt. If God were to act in justice untempered by mercy, everyone would be damned without hope. Wesley also saw the sins in terms of captivity, saying that, as sinners, "we are already bound hand and foot by the chains of our own sins."[58] He also called them wounds and diseases, but in relation to God, they are as debts beyond anyone's ability to pay, first and foremost.

Wesley writes that "the word translated *forgive* implies either to forgive a debt, or to unloose a chain,"[59] likewise applying to both images of sin mentioned above. The two are related, insofar as when God forgives the debt of sinners, he also releases them from the bondage of sin, in both the sin itself and also the guilt it brings. Furthermore, those who are forgiven are "in favour with God,"[60] and experience sanctification and righteousness.

The second half of the fifth petition, "as we forgive them that trespass against us," does not "denote the meritorious cause of our pardon; but the removal of that hindrance which otherwise would render it impossible."[61] He describes it as indicating both "on what condition, and in what degree

---

53. Wesley, "Sermon 26," 339.
54. Wesley, "Sermon 26," 339.
55. Wesley, "Sermon 26," 339.
56. Wesley, *Explanatory Notes*, 270.
57. Wesley, "Sermon 26," 339.
58. Wesley, "Sermon 26," 339.
59. Wesley, "Sermon 26," 339.
60. Wesley, "Sermon 26," 340.
61. Wesley, *Explanatory Notes*, 270.

or manner, we may look to be forgiven of God."[62] The conditional aspect is emphasized when Christ reiterates it a few verses later (Matt 6:14–15) and spells out that refusing to forgive others precludes receiving any forgiveness from God. The aspect of degree or manner emphasizes the importance of forgiving "from the heart," and not half-heartedly, as failure in this will "cut short the forgiveness of our own."[63] Furthermore, failing to forgive fully makes one's prayers to God for forgiveness an expression of "open defiance" in which "we are daring him to do his worst."[64] Wesley extrapolates this petition into a more extended form: "Give us, O Lord, redemption in thy blood, even the forgiveness of sins: as thou enablest us freely and fully to forgive every man, so do thou forgive all our trespasses."[65] This succinctly expresses Wesley's own understanding of what the fifth petition is requesting.

The sixth and final petition of the Lord's Prayer is "and lead us not into temptation, but deliver us from evil." Wesley comments that the Greek word translated "temptation" could also be translated "trial" and refer to any sort of difficulty, not just to a solicitation to evil. Narrowly speaking, this is not to be understood in the strictly active sense, because God certainly does not tempt people with evil (Jas 1:13–14). In this case, the petition should be understood as a request for God "not to suffer us to be led into it."[66]

Wesley understands the word "evil" in this phrase, based on the Greek, to refer "unquestionably [to] *the wicked one*."[67] Taking the petition in an optimistic sense—that is, with the expectation that God will, in fact, deliver us from Satan—he says, "All those who are children of God by faith are delivered out of his hands."[68] Thus, the Christian can pray this petition with the utmost confidence.

If Wesley understood these six petitions to encompass all requests a Christian could, in good conscience, ask of God,[69] his explanations seem to depict them as fairly comprehensive. It would be difficult to find a request that does not fit within these six petitions that would nevertheless fit

---

62. Wesley, "Sermon 26," 340.
63. Wesley, "Sermon 26," 340.
64. Wesley, "Sermon 26," 340.
65. Wesley, *Explanatory Notes*, 26.
66. Wesley, "Sermon 26," 341.
67. Wesley, "Sermon 26," 341.
68. Wesley, "Sermon 26," 341.
69. Wesley, "Sermon 26," 332.

Wesley's injunction not to "cover, stifle, or keep in [one's] desires, as if they were either too small or too great."[70]

The Lord's Prayer: Doxology

The third and last part of the Lord's Prayer is the doxology. This is "a solemn thanksgiving" and "a compendious acknowledgement of the attributes and works of God."[71] In the four phrases of this conclusion, Wesley found a summary and recapitulation in praise of the nature and majesty of God.

The first phrase, "For thine is the kingdom," speaks of God's "sovereign right [over] all things that are or ever were created."[72] The second phrase, "and the power," speaks of God's governing power throughout all of his kingdom.[73] The third phrase, "and the glory," speaks of "the praise due [God] from every creature."[74] These attributes belong to God "forever and ever" because he is the eternal God.

Conclusion

As a model prayer, Wesley saw in the Lord's Prayer everything necessary for a theological foundation for praying, instructions on what to pray for, and direction in praise and thanksgiving. It is an important source of insight into these aspects of Wesley's theology of prayer. Of it he says, "And this prayer uttered from the heart, and in its true and full meaning, is indeed the badge of a real Christian."[75] The very perfection of its model may have contributed to the struggle Wesley experienced in accepting extempore prayer, and later, trying to find a balance in the tension between prayer with and without forms.

---

70. Wesley, *Explanatory Notes*, 513.
71. Wesley, "Sermon 26," 341.
72. Wesley, "Sermon 26," 341.
73. Wesley, "Sermon 26," 341–42.
74. Wesley, "Sermon 26," 342.
75. Wesley, *Explanatory Notes*, 169.

— 6 —

Prayer with Forms and Without

IN HIS THEOLOGICAL DEVELOPMENT, John Wesley explored the tension between formal written prayers and extemporary prayer. This chapter examines how he began with the Book of Common Prayer and continued exploring written forms of prayer with his *Manuscript Prayer Book* (1730–34) and his first published work, the *Collection of Forms of Prayer for Every Day in the Week* (1733). From here, he began to experiment with other types of prayer, including especially extempore prayer. The experiments culminated in his revision of the Book of Common Prayer for Methodists in America, the *Sunday Service* (1784), which found space for both formal written prayers and extempore prayers in its liturgy. The *Sunday Service* represents the lasting balance that Wesley ultimately achieved, recognizing that prayers both with forms and without were necessary for prayer to be the growth of the healthy Christian life.

The Book of Common Prayer

The first Book of Common Prayer was published in 1549, with revisions published in 1552, 1559, 1604, and finally 1662 (which remains the "official" prayer book, despite periodic revisions, even in the twenty-first century). Although Wesley was raised on this last version, he showed a decided preference for the original 1549 version in some areas. He reverted to using the earlier edition from time to time, in general because he preferred its shorter, more direct language than that of the later revisions.[1]

The prayer book is not merely a collection of prayers. It contains the order of worship for morning and evening prayer, Communion, baptism, confirmation, marriage, visitation, and burial, as well as the Athanasian Creed, a catechism, the Psalter, and the Anglican Articles of Religion. It contains a calendar and table of Psalms and Scripture passages and the days on which each are to be read. In this manner, all the Scriptures would be consistently read in every church, year round. Prayers are, however, a central feature of the prayer book, and the book includes prayers for all occasions. Because of this, the prayer book was used by educated lay people for personal devotions and family religious instruction. In short, the prayer book was an all-purpose guide to Anglican spirituality.

As a child growing up in a staunchly Anglican household, the Book of Common Prayer formed the spirituality of much of John Wesley's early life. Later, as an ordained priest in the Anglican Church, the prayer book never lost its central place of importance in his public services or private devotions. Selleck demonstrates that throughout his adult life, Wesley followed prayer book rites nearly every Sunday that he was at his home base in London.[2] Furthermore, he frequently preached on the scriptural lessons that were on the prayer book calendar, although Anglican priests were given freedom to choose their own texts.[3] Finally, he testified numerous times in his journal to the emotional uplift and spiritual edification he received from reading prayers, reading the Scripture texts, partaking of Communion, and participating in the liturgy as a whole.[4]

The most thorough treatment of the role of the Book of Common Prayer in the life of Wesley is Selleck's unpublished 1983 dissertation "The Book of Common Prayer in the Theology of John Wesley." It delves into the various liturgies, the Eucharist, church discipline, and other related topics. The focus in this chapter, however, is on the role of the Book of Common Prayer in Wesley's prayer life and understanding of prayer. The most obvious influence the prayer book had on Wesley is that it taught him to pray exclusively through prewritten prayers, almost always the collects (short-form prayers) and longer prayers in the prayer book. These prayers—for

1. See Selleck, "Common Prayer," 76, 116, and 182.
2. Selleck, "Common Prayer," 84–86.
3. Selleck, "Common Prayer," 86–88.
4. Selleck, "Common Prayer," 88–90.

each week of the year, for special occasions, and for special needs—influenced Wesley's theology and his prayers for the rest of his life.

One of the places where the prayer book's influence is clear is Wesley's sermons. Selleck points out that the prayer of consecration, used in the Communion service, is echoed in several of Wesley's sermons.[5] In his sermon "Justification by Faith" Wesley says that Christ overcame sin and restored humanity to everlasting life "by that one oblation of himself, once offered, he hath redeemed me and all mankind; having thereby 'made a full, perfect, and sufficient sacrifice and satisfaction for the sins of the whole world.'"[6] This clearly echoes the opening lines of the prayer of consecration: "Almighty God, our heavenly Father, who of thy tender mercy didst give thine only Son Jesus Christ to suffer death upon the cross for our redemption; who made there (by his one oblation of himself once offered) a full, perfect, and sufficient sacrifice, oblation, and satisfaction for the sins of the whole world."[7] In his sermon "God's Love to Fallen Man"[8] Wesley quotes these words from the prayer of consecration to argue that Christ's self-sacrifice "is the 'greatest instance' of God's love."[9] In his sermon "Spiritual Worship" Wesley says God revealed himself as "the Redeemer of all the children of men" through that "one oblation of himself once offered, when he tasted death for every man, he might make a full and sufficient sacrifice, oblation, and satisfaction for the sins of the whole world."[10] Wesley explains Rom 10:4 in his sermon "The Righteousness of Faith," using the phrases of the prayer of consecration: "They were ignorant that 'Christ is the end of the law for righteousness to every one that believeth;'—that, by the oblation of himself once offered, he had put an end to the first law or covenant."[11] Although quotes and phrases from the prayer book are found throughout his sermons, they especially occur at the sermons' ends.

By Selleck's count, "ten of Wesley's sermons end with allusions to, paraphrases of, or quotations from the prayer book."[12] He especially notes

---

5. Selleck, "Common Prayer," 322–24.

6. Wesley, "Sermon 5," 55.

7. Book of Common Prayer (1662 edition), unnumbered page facing page U3, pointed out in Selleck, "Common Prayer," 322–23.

8. Wesley, "Sermon 59," 234.

9. Selleck, "Common Prayer," 323.

10. Wesley, "Sermon 77," 428, pointed out in Selleck, "Common Prayer," 323.

11. Wesley, "Sermon 6," 66.

12. Selleck, "Common Prayer," 332.

that Wesley concludes his sermon "Of Good Angels" with the collect for September 29, the Feast of St. Michael and All Angels:[13] "O everlasting God, who hast ordained and constituted the services of angels and men in a wonderful manner; grant that as thy holy angels always do thee service in heaven, so by thy appointment they may succour and defend us on earth, through Jesus Christ our Lord."[14]

Wesley's Manuscript Prayer Book

Wesley's fondness for written prayers was not confined to the official prayer book. From 1730 to 1734, Wesley assembled a notebook of nearly 250 prayers and collects and 60 poetic renderings of psalms that he came across in his spiritual reading, especially the Book of Common Prayer. He organized them largely according to Robert Nelson's schema in his book *Practice of True Devotion*, based on the days of the week.[15] Sunday was focused on "love of God," Monday was focused on "love of neighbor," Tuesday was focused on "humility," Wednesday was focused on "meekness, sweetness, and resignation," Thursday was focused on "sincerity and courtesy," and Friday was focused on "mortification." Nelson's original plan had Saturday focused on "chastity," but Wesley left Saturdays without a specific focus. However, he followed the Saturday prayers with a section titled, "For Those Who Live a Single Life," and included prayers on chastity. He collected all these prayers and psalms for personal use during morning and evening prayer.[16] Later, he may very well have shared his collection with his friends and the students he was tutoring at Lincoln College, but its format (in shorthand) was "ill-suited for more public use."[17] This led directly to the preparation and publication of his *Collection of Forms of Prayer*.

---

13. Selleck, "Common Prayer," 333.
14. Wesley, "Sermon 71," 370.
15. Wesley, *Manuscript Prayer Manual*, iii.
16. Wesley, *Manuscript Prayer Manual*, ii.
17. Wesley, *Manuscript Prayer Manual*, iii.

Wesley's *Collection of Forms of Prayer*

In 1733, Wesley published his first work, *Collection of Forms of Prayer for Every Day in the Week* for the use of his students.[18] Structurally, the book consists of three parts per day: the morning prayer, the evening prayer, and the self-examination questions. Thematically, the evening prayers largely follow the emphases used in his manuscript prayer journal, with Sunday focusing on "love of God," Monday on "love of neighbor," Tuesday on "humility," Wednesday and Friday on "mortification," Thursday on "resignation and meekness," and Saturday on "thankfulness." These emphases were chosen quite consciously. In the preface to the book, Wesley explains that the purpose was "to have such forms for those days which the Christian Church has ever judged peculiarly proper for religious rejoicing, as contained little of deprecation, but were explicit and large in acts of love and thanksgiving" as well as "to have such for those days which from the age of the Apostles have been set apart for religious mourning, as contained little of thanksgiving, but were full and express in acts of contrition and humiliation."[19] Johnson points out that the self-examination questions largely reflect the thematic content in the evening prayer of the day.[20]

Although *Forms of Prayer* predates Wesley's Aldersgate experience by five years, he continued to have the book reprinted and sold throughout his life. Part of the reason for its longevity is the sources he used. Besides the Bible, it draws liberally from the language and prayers of the Book of Common Prayer.

Selleck finds numerous echoes of the prayer book in Wesley's *Forms of Prayer*, and analyzes three prayers in particular. In the Wednesday evening prayer, for instance, Selleck analyzes the language and concludes that Wesley "constructed the first paragraph from the communion confession."[21] He points out the similarities between Wesley's Friday morning prayer and the prayer book's Kyrie, eleison ("Lord, have mercy on me") and the Sanctus: "As a takeoff on the Kyrie, this section relates the passion to 'me,' 'Have mercy on me.' The Sanctus is used as a starting point to contrast 'my' unworthiness to God's glory."[22] Finally, he recognizes the similarities

---

18. Wesley to John Newton, May 14, 1765, 299.
19. Wesley, Preface to "Collection," 77.
20. Johnson, "Liturgical Theology," 75.
21. Selleck, "Common Prayer," 179.
22. Selleck, "Common Prayer," 180.

between the Grand Litany of the prayer book and the Friday evening prayer: "The Friday evening prayer begins much as does the Litany, calling on each person of the Trinity to 'have mercy upon me,' and owns the Trinity as one God. . . . The prayer ends with an ascription to the Trinity as do many of the prayer book collects."[23] These are the most obvious instances of the prayer book influencing Wesley's *Forms of Prayer*.

Wesley's *Forms of Prayer* has other influences from the prayer book, however, that are not so obvious, as Selleck notes: "Subtle and often hidden phrases from the prayer book further connect one's private devotion to the corporate worship of the Church. For example, in the prayer for Friday evening, Jesus is petitioned to give grace that 'all who are redeemed by thy blood [may] *acknowledge thee to be the Lord*' (p. 232). The words in italics open the Te Deum in morning prayer."[24]

Selleck concludes that the overall effect of depending so heavily on prayer book material for the *Forms of Prayer* was that the reader's private prayers are linked "with the long tradition of the catholic Church."[25] Furthermore, certain uses of the prayer book materials may accomplish additional purposes. One such purpose was to "relate corporate experience to private life."[26] One of the ways Wesley achieves this in his book is through the thanksgivings. "Thanksgivings for the means of grace echo the General Thanksgiving of the established Church and connect personal religion to the Church's worship."[27] Each prayer was written to contain "something of deprecation, petition, thanksgiving, and intercession," which elsewhere he identifies as the "four grand parts of public prayer."[28] Each prayer was also written "to have intercessions every day for all those whom our own Church directs us to remember in our prayers."[29] As a group, the prayers were intended to comprise "the whole scheme of our Christian duty."[30] Wesley lays out this Christian duty under five points: self-renunciation, devotion to God, self-denial, mortification, and "Christ liveth in me."[31]

---

23. Selleck, "Common Prayer," 180.
24. Selleck, "Common Prayer," 316.
25. Selleck, "Common Prayer," 316.
26. Selleck, "Common Prayer," 316.
27. Selleck, "Common Prayer," 316.
28. Wesley, *Minutes of Conferences*, 59.
29. Wesley, Preface to "Collection," 77.
30. Wesley, Preface to "Collection," 77.
31. Wesley, Preface to "Collection," 77–78.

Experimental Prayer

Although forms of prayer were a great love of Wesley, he also experimented with both ejaculatory prayer and wordless prayer. Ejaculatory prayers were "short prayers or 'ejaculations' of praise or petition, often focusing on the main virtues; used hourly."[32] During the 1700s, "the habit of devout ejaculations was common among English mystics. Books of pious ejaculations were published."[33] Nehemiah Curnock, on the basis of Wesley's Oxford diary, argued that at some point during his time there, but "long before the formation of the Holy Club,"[34] Wesley began using ejaculatory prayer. Selleck recorded that the Oxford Methodists "used ejaculations for humility, faith, hope, and love."[35] Tuttle remarks that some think that "Wesley perfected the practice of ejaculatory prayer"[36] during his time at Wroot. At any rate, his use of them waxed and waned, but a note in his diary of December 9, 1735 reads, "No Hourly Prayers like Ejaculations!"[37] This suggests that he found them a continuing source of supernatural grace even as his circumstances and spiritual outlook changed.

According to Tuttle, "Mystics frequently abandoned all forms of prayer except for these periodic ejaculations. Since their lives were spent in the attitude of prayer, they saw no real need for formal prayer."[38] Indeed, as Wesley became more enamored of mysticism, he experimented with wordless prayer. "I grew acquainted with the Mystic writers, whose noble descriptions of union with God and internal religion made everything else appear mean, flat, and insipid."[39] "Public prayer, or any forms, they need not; for they pray without ceasing."[40]

Having embraced contemplative prayer, Wesley followed the lead of the mystics away from formal prayer. This led quickly into Quietism, the abandonment of the means of grace, which Wesley eventually rejected as unbiblical. "I think the rock on which I had nearest made shipwreck

---

32. Heitzenrater, "Editorial Introduction," 309.
33. Wesley, *Journal* (Curnock) 127.
34. Wesley, *Journal* (Curnock) 127.
35. Selleck, "Common Prayer," 71.
36. Tuttle, *Mysticism*, 73.
37. Wesley, *Journal* (Curnock) 127 (December 9, 1735).
38. Tuttle, *Mysticism*, 73.
39. Wesley, *Journal* (Curnock) 420 (January 25, 1738).
40. Wesley to Samuel Wesley Jr., November 23, 1736, 208.

of the faith was in the writings of the Mystics; under which term I comprehend all, and only those, who slight any of the means of grace."[41] He realized that abandoning formal vocal prayer for a wordless "attitude of prayer" was almost the same as abandoning prayer itself. "It is certain the Scripture by 'prayer' almost always means vocal prayer. And whosoever intermits this for any time will neither pray with the voice nor the heart."[42] He warned those who practiced the "presence of God" that "it is very possible . . . that you may insensibly slide into Quietism, [and] may become less zealous of good works."[43]

Later in his life he also realized that despite its potential for abuse, wordless communion with God was a real and valuable form of prayer, though not exclusive of verbal prayer, either through forms or extempore. In 1769, he writes, "At some times it is needful to say, 'I will pray with the Spirit and with the understanding also.' At other times the understanding has little to do, while the soul is poured forth in passive prayer."[44] Two years later, he tells a correspondent, "Temporal business need not interrupt your communion with God, though it varies the manner of it."[45] Three years after that, he writes, "There is no exercise more profitable to the soul than that of the presence of God. It is likewise of great use constantly and invariably to attend to His inward voice."[46] Wesley saw both the rewards and pitfalls of wordless prayer.

Extempore Prayer

Extemporary prayers were extremely uncommon among Anglicans of Wesley's time. Selleck explained that, at the Savoy Conference in 1661, "the Anglican *via media* had hardened into its own peculiar form of extremism in regard to the Book of Common Prayer. Insisting on forms of prayer, the Church's representatives would allow no room in the liturgy for extemporary prayer alongside the prayer book forms."[47] Although Dissenters used extemporary prayer, Wesley's exposure to them seems to have been minimal. His

41. Wesley to Samuel Wesley Jr., November 23, 1736, 207.
42. Wesley to Mary Bishop, September 19, 1773, 44.
43. Wesley to Ann Bolton, October 1, 1774, 115.
44. Wesley to Miss March, August 12, 1769, 147.
45. Wesley to Philothea Briggs, November 3, 1771, 286.
46. Wesley to Ann Bolton, October 1, 1774, 115.
47. Selleck, "Common Prayer," 29-30.

surprise at hearing an extemporary prayer among the Scottish immigrants at Darien in Georgia has already been recounted in the first chapter of this book, as well as his subsequent softening toward the idea in the days leading up to his Aldersgate experience. In addition, his journals record that a few months after his exposure to extemporary prayer at Darien, he himself prayed extempore, after some prompting: "I preached twice at Ponpon Chapel . . . and before the morning sermon (as Mr. Thompson had desired, [a] great part of the congregation being Dissenters) used an extempore prayer."[48] Selleck concludes that Wesley "owed his own experimentation with extemporary prayer to [the Puritans]."[49]

These experiments were evidently successful. Extemporary prayer came to characterize the revival under Wesley and the practice of prayer of the Methodists. In 1755, Wesley writes, "Neither dare I confine myself wholly to forms of prayer, not even in the Church. I use, indeed, all the forms; but I frequently add extemporary prayer either before or after sermon."[50] However, he clearly had been doing more than simply adding extemporary prayer before or after the sermon. Extemporary prayer made its way more deeply into the liturgy. "When they began to hold communion services in Methodist chapels, it seemed natural that both hymns and extemporary prayer, two meaningful aspects of society meetings and of the Revival, would find their way into the Communion service."[51] By 1745, Wesley had made these changes. "Within the framework of the Order for Holy Communion of the Book of Common Prayer, the Wesleys inserted hymns and concluded with extemporary prayer."[52] In addition, "extemporary prayer came to occupy an important position in the Lord's Supper. . . . [It] occurred at three possible points in the Eucharist: before or after the sermon, during the sermon, and after the Gloria at the close of the service."[53] Extemporary prayer was now a prominent part of the Methodist movement.

In making these changes, Wesley was clearly departing from the Anglican norm. "His use of hymns and extemporary prayer, while perhaps not an infringement on rubric, also marked his liturgical practices as unusual

---

48. Wesley, *Journal* (Curnock) 351 (April 24, 1737).
49. Selleck, "Common Prayer," 184.
50. Wesley to Samuel Walker, November 20, 1755, 152.
51. Selleck, "Common Prayer," 125.
52. Selleck, "Common Prayer," 125.
53. Selleck, "Common Prayer," 126.

and irregular."⁵⁴ Wesley acknowledges that one of the ways the Methodists were considered "irregular" was by their "frequently using extemporary prayer."⁵⁵ Wesley came under repeated criticism for this, some from his own brother, Samuel, who told him to "banish extemporary expositions and extemporary prayers."⁵⁶ Wesley defends his practice, explaining how he first came to use extemporary prayer: "I believed [extemporary prayer] to be my bounden duty, for the sake of those who desired me to watch over their souls. I could not in conscience refrain from it."⁵⁷ More criticism came from other sources.

One man tried to refute extemporary prayer by arguing that one could not both think and pray at the same time. Wesley retorted that by the same logic, one could not read and pray at the same time, either.⁵⁸ A correspondent argued, writing, "If you suppose the Scripture enjoins you to use extemporary prayer, then you must suppose our Liturgy to be inconsistent with Scripture; and, consequently, unlawful to be used."⁵⁹ To this, Wesley replies, "That does not follow; unless I supposed the Scripture to enjoin, to use extemporary prayer and no other. Then it would follow, that a form of prayer was inconsistent with Scripture. But this I never did suppose."⁶⁰ Wesley defended extemporary prayer because he thought it was good, useful, conducive to increased righteousness, and therefore worth defending. "His use of extemporary prayer contradicted no canon that he knew of, but he also insisted that obedience to any canon depended on its consistency with the Word of God."⁶¹ Because of this, Wesley both used and defended extemporary prayer.

The mature Wesley could acknowledge, "I often use extemporary prayer."⁶² But if he faced criticism from those within the Anglican Church who took umbrage, he also recognized the limitations of extempore prayer and the importance of forms. He confesses in a letter, "But, to speak freely, I myself find more life in the Church prayers than in the formal

54. Selleck, "Common Prayer," 135–36.
55. Wesley, *Minutes of Conferences*, 58.
56. Samuel Wesley Jr. to John Wesley, April 16, 1739.
57. Wesley, "Farther Thoughts," 272.
58. Wesley, *Works* (Bicentennial) 19:173 (October 28, 1740).
59. Wesley, "Principles Farther Explained," 438.
60. Wesley, "Principles Farther Explained," 438.
61. Selleck, "Common Prayer," 140.
62. Wesley, "Principles Farther Explained," 444.

extemporary prayers of Dissenters."[63] His friend Abraham Jones explains to him in a 1742 letter why he used forms instead of extempore prayer: "The lame must use crutches till they can go without."[64] Wesley evidently agreed with his sentiment, and says in his sermon "Catholic Spirit," "It appears to me, that forms of prayer are of excellent use, particularly in the great congregation. If you judge extemporary prayer to be of more use, act suitably to your own judgment."[65] As easygoing as this sounds, however, Wesley also pushed prayer with forms.

Wesley anticipated that a full switch to extempore prayer would tend to separate the Methodists from the Church of England, and Wesley by all means wanted to avoid that. He writes, "By our reading prayers we prevent our people's contracting an hatred for forms of prayer, which would naturally be the case if we always prayed extempore."[66] Later, he elaborated more fully that if he or his brother were ill, "I desired one of our other preachers . . . to preach . . . after reading part of the Church Prayers. This both my brother and I judged would endear the Church Prayers to them; whereas, if they were used wholly to extemporary prayer, they would naturally contract a kind of contempt if not aversion to forms of prayer: so careful were we from the beginning to prevent their leaving the Church."[67] In short, he writes, "I concur in the judgement of my brother that the using of the form of prayer will tend to unite our people to the Church [of England] rather than to separate them from it."[68] Wesley was always loyal to the Church of England, and tried to encourage his Methodists to be loyal as well.

Beyond the forms of prayer in the prayer book, which would serve his purposes to unite the Methodists more closely with the Church of England, Wesley continued to recommend forms of prayer not found in the prayer book. For instance, Selleck points out that Wesley's *Christian Library*, which reprinted (and abridged) works of divinity Wesley approved for reading, regularly contained forms of prayer,[69] and that he used Matthew Henry's "Method of Family Prayer" "as a pattern for Methodist

---

63. Wesley to Miss Bishop, October 18, 1778, 326.
64. Jones to John Wesley, December 12, 1742, 150.
65. Wesley, "Sermon 39," 499.
66. Wesley to William Percival, February 17, 1787, 370.
67. Wesley to the Printer of the *Dublin Chronicle*, June 2, 1789, 141.
68. Wesley to William Thom, June 21, 1790, 223.
69. Selleck, "Common Prayer," 177.

family worship."[70] Of course, in addition to all this, Wesley revised the prayer book for the Methodists in North America.

Wesley's *Sunday Service*

In 1784, Wesley published his *Sunday Service of the Methodists in North America*. This book was essentially a revision of the Book of Common Prayer. Many of the revisions were cuts in the material. As a result of these cuts, Wesley's *Sunday Service* wound up being half the size of the prayer book.[71] The section of Psalms was reduced from the full Psalter to a mere selection for use in his thirty-day plan of morning and evening readings, and much of that reduction was for theological reasons, as he explains in a letter: "Many Psalms [are] left out, and many parts of the others, as being highly improper for the mouths of a Christian Congregation."[72] References to Epiphany and Lent were also removed but, oddly, the lessons for those seasons were retained.[73] Other noticeable cuts included the removal of the Athanasian Creed, the catechism, and the order for confirmation, and Thanksgiving for Women after Childbearing.[74] Many of the revisions he made impacted the practice of prayer among those who used it.

The overall shape of the *Sunday Service* is laid out in an introductory letter Wesley wrote. In describing the liturgy he had prepared, Wesley writes, "I advise all the travelling preachers to use [it] on the Lord's day in all the congregations, reading the litany only on Wednesdays and Fridays, and praying extempore on all other days."[75] This was a significant change from the prayer book, which expected the liturgical morning and evening prayers to be read every day. In Wesley's *Sunday Service*, morning and evening prayer (along with the Lord's Supper) was done only on Sunday.

Wesley not only reduced the number of prayers (cutting, for instance, the concluding collects from five down to two), but also the well-known, classical prayers.[76] "It is ironic that although Wesley claimed to hold Scripture and the Early Church as normative, he chose to eliminate all

---

70. Selleck, "Common Prayer," 109.
71. Wade, "Public Worship," 24.
72. Wesley, *Sunday Service*, A2.
73. Selleck, "Common Prayer," 190.
74. Baker, *Church of England*, 244.
75. Wesley to "Our Brethren in America," September 10, 1784, 239.
76. Wade, "Public Worship," 33.

the classic biblical canticles or hymns of the classic daily office, the Venite, Benedictus, Benedicite, Magnificat, and Nunc Dimittis, retaining only the Te Deum and selections from the Psalter."[77] As a result of this, the balance of the daily office changed. "The elements of confession, prayers and the amount of reading from the Scriptures remains basically the same. The most substantial loss is that of praise and petition."[78]

The daily office was not the only victim of Wesley's cutting. The Communion service also had several notable changes. "As in the orders for Morning and Evening Prayer, Wesley replaces the priestly absolution of sins with a pastoral prayer for the forgiveness of sins for those who have repented with faith."[79] Another change came in the general confession of sins, wherein "Wesley omits the phrase 'the burden of them is intolerable to us' concerning sins confessed by the faithful. This would be in keeping with Wesley's doctrine of Christian assurance."[80] Finally, "One major revision of the text is Wesley's cutting of the prayer of thanksgiving after the communion by half and the provision for *ex tempore* prayer at the end of the service."[81] The presence of extempore prayer, here in the Communion service and throughout the *Sunday Service*, is a significant departure from the prayer book and one of the defining features of the *Sunday Service*.

Horton Davies, after a careful analysis, came to the conclusion that "the essence of Methodist worship as it germinated in the fertile mind of its founder was the combination of the advantages of liturgical forms and of free prayers."[82] It was the combination of the two that made his approach to religion so uniquely strong, as well as historically important. In fact, Davies believes that "this combination of a convinced High Churchman's appreciation of liturgy and the Eucharist with a practical if reluctant recognition of the value of extemporary preaching, free prayer, and hymns made Wesley's liturgical contributions the most important single fact in the history of English Christianity in the eighteenth century."[83]

Wesley's balance between liturgical and extempore prayer looked decidedly unbalanced to some commentators. William Nash Wade felt it

---

77. Wade, "Public Worship," 34.
78. Wade, "Public Worship," 35.
79. Wade, "Public Worship," 84.
80. Wade, "Public Worship," 85.
81. Wade, "Public Worship," 85.
82. Davies, *Worship and Theology*, 184.
83. Davies, *Worship and Theology*, 184–85.

necessary "to stress, especially in the light of subsequent American Methodist liturgical piety, John Wesley's high regard for the Book of Common Prayer and his acceptance and support of its printed prayer forms and texts."[84] He later comments, "Thus, while John Wesley would advocate and practice the use of *ex tempore* prayer in contrast to employing only the authorized public prayers in the *Book of Common Prayer*, we should remember . . . that such *ex tempore* prayer was to be *in addition to* and serve as a *supplement* to the accustomed *Book of Common Prayer* texts and forms."[85] He goes on to emphasize that this was not to be understood "as a complete replacement of the established common liturgy. For John Wesley, the question concerning *ex tempore* prayer and printed common liturgical prayers was never 'Either/or' but 'Both/and.'"[86]

Wesley's notes (that is, his journal, diaries, and letters) leave no hint at the process of revision that produced the *Sunday Service*.[87] To identify a rationale for his revisions, one must look elsewhere. Horton Davies's analysis of Wesleyan worship reveals that "Wesley's theory of worship emphasizes the notes of simplicity, obedience, and edification. Ceremonial for its own sake is a distraction; the Christian's attendance at worship may be a privilege, but it is certainly a duty and a homage to the Divine king; and its benefit is that the worshippers may be built up in the faith and into holiness and love."[88] One of the main goals for revising the prayer book, then, was to streamline it and make it simpler, which would certainly explain cutting its size by almost half.

Another reason for the changes Wesley made was the cultural differences between Anglicans and American Methodists. For instance, their secular government was different. "Wesley was careful to remove any mention of the word 'King' from any prayers in the 1784 *Sunday Service*, substituting instead the phrase 'the supreme rulers.'"[89] Religious and theological expectations were different in North America. In attempting to explain the reduction in holy days Wesley made for the *Sunday Service*, Wade says that "exactly how much the attitude of the American Methodists or at least Wesley's understanding of their opinions shaped this part of

---

84. Wade, "Public Worship," 16.
85. Wade, "Public Worship," 17.
86. Wade, "Public Worship," 17.
87. Wade, "Public Worship," 22.
88. Davies, *Worship and Theology*, 197.
89. Wade, "Public Worship," 65.

the revision cannot be definitely ascertained."[90] Despite this, he still argues that "Wesley was most likely correct in believing a warm reception of such 'Holy days' by American Methodists was not to be counted upon."[91] In the Communion service, he replaced the declaration of absolution with a pastoral prayer for forgiveness, and in doing so, "he expressed a doctrinal position different from the Church of England and one which would find wide acceptance among American Methodists."[92] Wesley was sensitive to the cultural differences of American Methodists, and sought to accommodate them when he could.

The last major reason for Wesley's revisions was theology. For instance, the prayer book contained many readings from the Apocrypha, but Wesley eliminated the daily office calendar and the sanctoral readings from the prayer book, leaving the *Sunday Service* with only a *single sentence* from the Apocrypha (from the Book of Tobit).[93] On Wesley's elimination of Lent, Wade theorizes that "both Ash Wednesday with its emphasis upon the reconciliation of penitents and the rest of Lent whose lengthy period of fasting and repentance in preparation for baptism would have been at odds with Wesley's doctrine of Christian assurance and the peace and joy and forgiveness which belongs to a faithful believing Christian."[94] Johnson arrives at a different explanation: "[Wesley] believed Lent to be superfluous. Wesley believed and taught that fasting was a primary means of grace, and challenged his people to fast at least twice a week."[95] Both explanations fit what is known about Wesley, and while each is a sufficient explanation for his decision to eliminate Lent on its own, the reality is that both explanations probably influenced his decision to some degree.

The Psalms, especially, were a target of his theological editing. Although Wesley's "Select Psalms" for the *Sunday Service* was reduced by about one-sixth the size of the full Psalter, this section still constituted over a third of the page count of the *Sunday Service*.[96] Wade engaged in a full analysis of each of the deleted psalms, and each emendation of included psalms, to arrive at the conclusion that psalms were edited to make them

90. Wade, "Public Worship," 41–42.
91. Wade, "Public Worship," 42.
92. Wade, "Public Worship," 35.
93. Wade, "Public Worship," 42–43.
94. Wade, "Public Worship," 45.
95. Johnson, "Liturgical Theology," 115–16.
96. Wade, "Public Worship," 54–55.

fit to be used in a literalistic fashion when sung or prayed by the American Methodists. When editing for content, Wesley cut descriptions of evil men, unique personal confessions, geographic references to Israel, references to kings, Old Testament worship practices, references to "works-righteousness," and to suppress references to instrumental worship.[97]

Lasting Balance

Wesley was raised to value the prayer book and set forms of prayer, but in close proximity to his Aldersgate experience, Wesley discovered the power of extempore prayer. He testifies that "my heart was so full that I could not confine myself to the forms of prayer which we were accustomed to use there. Neither do I purpose to be confined to them any more; but to pray indifferently, with a form or without, as I may find suitable to particular occasions."[98] Even here, however, there is no indication of a pendulum swinging from one extreme to the other. He had discovered the power of extempore prayer, and he intended to use it alongside his formal prayers. Selleck agrees with this assessment, saying, "Extemporary prayer was another early innovation. Wesley's own liturgical practice indicates that such prayer was not intended to replace forms of prayer. Instead, it brought to the liturgy a personal dimension and a life that had been lacking in Anglican formalism."[99] Wesley's development of extemporary prayer was a growth and expansion of his theology and practice of prayer, not merely a change.

Despite the power of extempore prayer, Wesley never lost sight of the value of forms of prayer, as Selleck notes: "Forms of prayer (and hymnody) became a means to teach and to reinforce the doctrines essential to Methodist devotion. Wesley's own forms of prayer, an amalgamation of Scripture, the prayer book, and other traditional sources, demonstrates that prayer was both dialogue with God and 'the school wherein the soul learneth to *know* God aright.'"[100] This hodgepodge, this eclectic assimilation of various sources, even sources as diametrically opposed as formal and extempore prayer, was part of the genius of Wesley. Davies comments on the results of this practice of amalgamation, "John Wesley was unique . . . in being the bridge that crossed the chasm between the worship of Anglicanism and

97. Wade, "Public Worship," 61–68.
98. Wesley, *Works* (Jackson) 1:90 (April 1, 1738).
99. Selleck, "Common Prayer," 338.
100. Selleck, "Common Prayer," 202.

Dissent. . . . His Catholic mind ranged through the centuries of Church history and raided its devotional treasures like an avid Christian Pirate."[101] The end result of Wesley's practical attitude toward Christian devotion was the enrichment of Methodist liturgy and spirituality.

Throughout the rest of his life and ministry, Wesley maintained this balance. Decades later, he could advise a correspondent, "A form of prayer used in private may be of considerable use; only now and then, at the beginning or middle or end of it, you may break out a little and speak a few words, just according to the present temper of your mind. When your sins are forgiven, you will surely be sensible of it; and 'every one that seeketh findeth.'"[102] Despite the value of extempore prayer, Selleck says that John Wesley "refused to do away with forms of prayer realizing that such an omission would not guarantee warmth, depth, or spontaneity, in public prayer."[103] One of the great values of set forms of prayer is their ability to enable "us to recall afterward what we have prayed for. Such prayers are to be offered up with an earnest and sincere desire for the good things of God."[104] Wesley saw the value of both types of prayer, and used them both.

Wesley's tenacity in retaining formal prayers is directly related to the strength of the Anglican prayer book. Throughout his life, he returned to the prayer book again and again, not only for personal spiritual strength, but also for directive and formative purposes in leading the Methodists. "Upon prayer book doctrine he defended Methodism as well as his loyalty to the Church. The use of extemporary prayer and hymns did not negate for him the value of that book; he used both to infuse prayer book rites with the spirit that was so lacking in the formalism typical of eighteenth century Anglicanism."[105]

Selleck identifies this formalism as one of the major pitfalls that Wesley sought to avoid with the Methodists: "Wesley used the Book of Common Prayer as a means to maintain a balanced religion. He combined the advantages of liturgical forms and free prayer. Although he used the liturgical forms of the Church of England, he avoided the pitfalls of formalism by introducing into the rite the use of hymns, extemporary prayer, and

---

101. Davies, *Worship and Theology*, 184.
102. Wesley to Abraham Orchard, January 1, 1783, 161.
103. Selleck, "Common Prayer," 301.
104. Selleck, "Common Prayer," 299.
105. Selleck, "Common Prayer," 143.

exhortation."[106] The other major pitfall Selleck identified is the opposite extreme of mysticism that denied the means of grace: "Insisting on prayer book orders, complemented by hymn-singing and extempore prayer, he protected Methodism, on the one hand, from the barren sacerdotalism of many Anglican priests and, on the other hand, from the negation of the means of grace by the Moravians and mystics."[107] The end result was the creation of something new: the Methodists. "The prescribed liturgy, modified by Wesley's revisions and the addition of extemporary prayer and hymns, gave form and content to Christian faith."[108] Selleck's analysis is similar to that of Knight.

Knight likewise saw a theologically complementary relationship between the formal written prayers of the prayer book and extemporary prayer, but his analysis was slightly different. He begins by noting that Wesley understood salvation as a relationship with God: "A relationship necessarily involves the *presence* of an other who has a distinctive *identity*."[109] This relationship is threatened by two extremes: the formalist who focuses on the identity of God without recognizing his presence, and the enthusiast who focuses on the presence of God without recognizing his identity. To thwart these two extremes, Wesley held to written forms of prayer alongside extempore prayer. "If prayer is the lifting of one's heart to God, the written prayers provide descriptive access to the God to whom one prays. If prayer is to be made at all times and in all places, extemporary prayer discerns the presence of God in particular contexts and brings the needs of each situation before God."[110]

In particular, the collects of the prayer book written by Thomas Cranmer, which Wesley kept in his *Sunday Service*, exemplified the power of written prayers in addressing the descriptive aspects of one's relationship to God because they "contain both scriptural descriptions of God and petitions warranted by those descriptions."[111] Knight argues that "to pray the collects over time is to become increasingly acquainted with who God is, and who God intends for us to be. The prayers of the church avoid enthusiasm through offering concrete scriptural descriptions of

106. Selleck, "Common Prayer," 159.
107. Selleck, "Common Prayer," 164.
108. Selleck, "Common Prayer," 341.
109. Knight, *Presence of God*, 11.
110. Knight, *Presence of God*, 120.
111. Knight, *Presence of God*, 162.

God, and thus evoke and shape affections, inform Christian practice, and provide language and direction for extemporaneous prayer."[112] Finally, Knight concludes that "prayer as descriptive identity and prayer focused on God's presence in concrete circumstances are mutually dependent and essential to an ongoing relationship with God; together they are one prayer to the one distinctive God who is present."[113] In using both types of prayer, Knight points out that Wesley unifies both relational elements of presence and identity.

Conclusion

In Wesley's developing understanding of prayer, he branched out from the formalist, written prayers of the Book of Common Prayer and his own *Manuscript Prayer Manual* and *Collection of Forms of Prayer*. He experimented with several other styles of prayer, eventually rejecting Quietist forms, but embracing extempore prayers as a complementary balance to his well-beloved written forms of prayer. These two types of prayer brought a lasting balance to his theology and practice of prayer as the growth of a healthy Christian life, a life that could be lived in harmony with other Christians in community.

---

112. Knight, *Presence of God*, 162.
113. Knight, *Presence of God*, 120.

— 7 —

Prayer and Community

John Wesley understood that prayer is practiced in community and affects people's relationships. This chapter examines the directions Wesley gave for the conduct of public prayer, in both preaching services and prayer meetings, and especially notes his watchfulness against "enthusiasm," religious fanaticism that resulted in disorderly and inappropriate praying. Next, this chapter looks at the family as a place for teaching children to pray. Both friendships and family relationships are of continuing importance to a believer's prayer life far beyond childhood, and marriage is an important element in this. Finally, this chapter examines the role of prayer in facing opposition, with reconciliation being the ultimate goal.

Public Praying

Preaching services were not the only opportunity for public prayer in Wesley's Methodist societies. Wesley also encouraged the organization of prayer meetings, as long as they did not replace or detract from public preaching: "I love prayer-meetings, and wish they were set up in every corner of the town. But I doubt whether it would be well to drop any of the times of preaching."[1] Unfortunately, some resulting prayer meetings were either poorly organized, poorly disciplined, or both. These sometimes

---

1. Wesley to Joseph Benson, December 11, 1772, 3.

caused more trouble than they were worth. He directed one of his preachers, "You did well to prevent all irregular and turbulent prayer-meetings."[2] On the other hand, even troublesome prayer meetings could be valuable. "Even irregular, ill-conducted prayer meetings have been productive of much good. But they will be productive of much more while they are kept under proper regulations."[3] To aid Adam Clarke in reforming some of the prayer meetings, he gave these directions: "I will give you a few direction[s]: (1) See that no prayer-meeting continue later than nine at night, particularly on Sunday. Let the house be emptied before the clock strikes nine. (2) Let there be no exhortation at any prayer-meeting. (3) Beware of jealousy or judging another. (4) Never think a man is an enemy to the work because he reproves irregularities."[4]

Whether in a preaching service or a prayer meeting, Wesley had a strong sense of what it took to pray well in public. His instructions pertaining to this are clear and unambiguous: "Nor is it expedient for any Methodist Preacher to imitate the Dissenters in their manner of praying; either in his tone,—all particular tones both in prayer and preaching should be avoided with the utmost care."[5] Wesley despised the histrionics and affectations that he saw in other (particularly Dissenting) pulpits. Such theatricality brought attention to the one praying at the expense of attention to God. He continues, "Nor in his language,—all his words should be plain and simple, such as the lowest of his hearers both use and understand; or in the length of his prayer, which should not usually exceed four or five minutes, either before or after sermon."[6] Wesley was ever mindful of his audience, especially in field preaching designed to reach those who would never darken a church door. People attending his meetings were frequently uneducated, and flowery language posed a barrier between them and the gospel message. Likewise, prayers of excessive length could tax the attention span of the congregation, take time away from the sermon, and tempt the one praying into showy self-indulgence.

Similar advice applied to the public reading of prayers. "It is no small advantage that the person who reads prayers, though not always the same, yet is always one who may be supposed to speak from his heart, one whose

2. Wesley to Adam Clarke, October 28, 1790, 244.
3. Wesley to Adam Clarke, October 31, 1789, 182.
4. Wesley to Adam Clarke, September 9, 1790, 237.
5. Wesley, "Reasons Against a Separation," 230.
6. Wesley, "Reasons Against a Separation," 230.

life is no reproach to his profession, and one who performs that solemn part of divine service, not in a careless, hurrying, slovenly manner, but seriously and slowly, as becomes him who is transacting so high an affair between God and man."[7] Here, Wesley emphasized the character of the one reading prayers. Sincerity and godliness prevent the accusations of hypocrisy that might undermine the message. An attitude of seriousness and solemnity, characterized by an unhurried attention to detail, communicate the momentous importance of going before the Lord in prayer.

Although a man particular with details, Wesley was nevertheless broad-minded enough to recognize the Spirit of God even when his standards may not have been met. "The fire kindled more and more, till Mrs. ———— asked if I would give her leave to pray. Such a prayer I never heard before: It was perfectly an original; odd and unconnected, made up of disjointed fragments, and yet like a flame of fire. Every sentence went through my heart, and I believe the heart of every one present. For many months I have found nothing like it. It was good for me to be here."[8] In this meeting, blessed by the presence of the Holy Spirit, one who probably would not meet at least some of Wesley's standards for regular public praying is nevertheless allowed by him to pray publicly. She is then used by God to bring blessing and spiritual edification, not only to the regular congregation, but even to Wesley himself, who testified to its power even several months later.

Enthusiasm

On the other hand, Wesley was emphatic in his disapproval of those who prayed in a style that he considered indicative of "enthusiasm." Chief among the characteristics of this style was an inappropriate familiarity with the Godhead in prayer and other failures to give due respect to the Most High. In speaking of some of the Calvinists, he asks, "Do they gather constant, universal self-denial, the patience of hope, the labour of love, inward and outward self-devotion . . . from that *amorous* way of praying to Christ or that way of preaching His righteousness? I never found it so."[9] To one of his societies, he offers a letter of correction for some of their excesses: "But I dislike several things therein: . . . the singing, or speaking, or praying, of several at once, . . . the using improper expressions in

---

7. Wesley to a Friend, September 20, 1757, 227.
8. Wesley, *Works* (Jackson) 3:196 (September 17, 1764).
9. Wesley to John Fletcher, March 20, 1768, 83.

prayer; sometimes too bold, if not irreverent; sometimes too pompous and magnificent, extolling yourselves rather than God, and telling him what you are, not what you want, . . . the never kneeling at prayer, . . . your using postures or gestures highly indecent, . . . your screaming, even so as to make the words unintelligible."[10]

Screaming in prayer was a problem that happened again and again. In 1762, John Wesley writes to his brother Charles Wesley: "Those who prayed were partly the occasion of this [disorder], by their horrid screaming, and unscriptural, enthusiastic expressions."[11] In 1786, John Wesley records of a congregation he visited: "But even while they are full of love, Satan strives to push many of them to extravagance. This appears in several instances:—1. Frequently three or four, yea, ten or twelve, pray aloud all together. 2. Some of them, perhaps many, scream all together as loud as they possibly can."[12] These were in addition to the other problems, including the aforementioned problem of over-familiarity in prayer: "3. Some of them use improper, yea, indecent expressions in prayer. 4. Several drop down as dead; and are as stiff as a corpse; but in a while they start up and cry, 'Glory! glory!' perhaps twenty times together. Just so did the French Prophets, and very lately the Jumpers in Wales, bring the real work into contempt."[13]

On one occasion, a negative report came to Wesley about the prayers George Bell was praying at the Foundry. In order to investigate, Wesley came secretly to a meeting there to observe. "Being determined to hear for myself, I stood where I could hear and see, without being seen. George Bell prayed, in the whole pretty near an hour. His fervour of spirit I could not but admire. I afterwards told him what I did not admire; namely, . . . his screaming, every now and then, in so strange a manner, that one could scarce tell what he said."[14] Despite the correction, Bell continued to pray in a manner unacceptable to Wesley, and he forbade Bell from praying at the Foundry. "I heard George Bell once more, and was convinced he must not continue to pray at the Foundry. The reproach of Christ I am willing to bear; but not the reproach of enthusiasm, if I can help it."[15] Wesley refused to approve of these disorderly innovations in prayer.

10. Wesley, *Works* (Jackson) 3:121 (November 2, 1762).
11. Wesley to Charles Wesley, December 11, 1762, 196.
12. Wesley, *Works* (Jackson) 4:329 (April 3, 1786).
13. Wesley, *Works* (Jackson) 4:329 (April 3, 1786).
14. Wesley, *Works* (Jackson) 3:122 (November 24, 1762).
15. Wesley, *Works* (Jackson) 3:124 (December 22, 1762).

One way of giving appropriate respect to God was to kneel during prayers. Kneeling during prayers was important to Wesley, and he mentioned it several times. His correction to his societies for not kneeling during prayer has already been cited (above). Numerous times the *Minutes of the Methodist Conferences* mention kneeling in prayer. For instance, part of the minutes of the 1752 Limerick conference read, "How shall we set an example to the people of decency in public worship? . . . (1) Let us constantly kneel during prayer; and stand both in singing, and while the text is repeating, &c. (2) Let us be serious and silent while service lasts, and when we are coming and going away."[16] The minutes for the 1786 conference read, "Exhort all to sing, and all to stand at singing, as well as to kneel at prayers."[17] In 1784, Wesley corrects a society at Tewksbury: "On my mentioning the impropriety of standing at prayer, and sitting while we were singing praise to God, they all took advice; kneeling while we prayed and stood up while we sung Psalms."[18] In 1780–89, the conference minutes again read, "Always kneel during public prayer."[19]

Outside of prayer meetings, Wesley was particular about the length of public prayers. He writes, "Therefore I have over and over advised, use no *long prayer*, either before or after sermon. Therefore I myself frequently use only a collect, and never enlarge in prayer, unless at intercession, or on a watch-night, or on some extraordinary occasion."[20] Exactly how long should one pray? In 1760, Wesley gave numbers: "Do not you stint your lay preachers to three or four minutes only in their public prayers? I advise them not usually to exceed four or five minutes either before or after sermon."[21] Nearly thirty years later, the minutes of the 1789 conference record, "Do not usually pray above eight or ten minutes (at most) without intermission."[22]

---

16. Wesley, *Minutes of Conferences*, 715.
17. Wesley, *Minutes of Conferences*, 194.
18. Wesley, *Works* (Jackson) 4:267 (March 17, 1784).
19. Wesley, *Minutes of Conferences*, 529.
20. Wesley, *Minutes of Conferences*, 59.
21. Wesley to Mr. T. H., etc., December 12, 1760, 122.
22. Wesley, *Minutes of Conferences*, 527.

Family Prayer

In between public and private prayer was family prayer. For Wesley, this was no mere afterthought. He had been raised in Susanna Wesley's exacting school of family discipleship, and family prayer was its central element.[23] Wesley, likewise, saw it as an important element in the overall structure of Methodist discipline, and encouraged it as such. This is seen most clearly in the minutes to the Methodist annual conferences. In 1763, the preachers are encouraged to "inquire in each house, Have you family-prayer? Do you read the Scripture in your family? Have you a fixed time for private prayer?"[24] Further, they are asked, "Do you use all the means of grace yourself, and enforce the use of them on all persons? . . . The instituted are, 1. Prayer; private, family, public; consisting of deprecation, petition, intercession, thanksgiving."[25] Here, family prayers are listed alongside private prayers and public prayers, and are included with them as the object of the subsequent question, "Do you use each of these constantly (at set times) and fervently?"[26] Later, a follow-up question asks, "Do you ask everywhere, . . . Have you family prayer?"[27] In 1765, the preachers are told, "Therefore strongly recommend, both in public and private, the having family-prayer, morning and evening, and after reading a chapter, and that in the most lively manner."[28] In 1766, they are told to "read, explain and enforce" Matthew Henry's "Method of Family Prayer."[29] Although Wesley published both *A Collection of Prayers for Families* and *Prayers for Children*, he does not seem to have thought of prayers as materially different when prayed by a child rather than an adult. In a letter, Wesley instructs, "In praying with the children, you have only to ask for those things which you are sensible they most want, and that in the most plain, artless, and simple language which you can devise."[30] Although methods and plans for family prayer might be helpful, the most important thing for Wesley was simply to do it.

---

23. See chapter 1 of this book.
24. Wesley, *Minutes of Conferences*, 456 ("Large" *Minutes*, 1763).
25. Wesley, *Minutes of Conferences*, 548 ("Large" *Minutes*, 1763).
26. Wesley, *Minutes of Conferences*, 548 ("Large" *Minutes*, 1763).
27. Wesley, *Minutes of Conferences*, 548 ("Large" *Minutes*, 1763).
28. Wesley, *Minutes of Conferences*, 53.
29. Wesley, *Minutes of Conferences*, 69.
30. Wesley to Mary Bishop, March 8, 1771, 227.

Friendship and Family

Wesley was keenly aware of the effect of prayer on human relationships, especially close relationships, and he frequently addressed the role of prayer in interpersonal interactions. Wesley knew the importance of having a close friend and confidant to support one in the Christian life. He had a number of close friends, as well as his brother, Charles Wesley. When Ann Bolton complained to John Wesley about her lack of friendship, he encouraged her to turn to prayer: "I wonder you do not find one person that knows how to sympathize with you. Surely there must be some such in the Society at Witney; although you have not yet found them, perhaps for want of praying for this very thing. I advise you to make it a matter of earnest prayer; and certainly God will give you a friend."[31] To Harriet Lewis, who had decided to be "not almost but altogether a Christian," Wesley writes a letter warning her that "if this be your determination, you must remember you cannot be warm alone; you must needs find one if not more with whom you can converse freely on the things of God."[32] He was not content merely to give orders, however; he encouraged her that "this you may properly make matter of prayer; and sooner or later your prayer will be heard."[33] Wesley was confident of God's desire to bring Christians into close relationship.

If finding a close Christian friend to support one in becoming "altogether a Christian" was important, at least equally important was dealing with less devoted, more worldly Christians who would distract one from the fullness of God's will. Wesley warns John Fletcher against "the genteel Methodists"[34] who were "salt that has lost its savour."[35] Instead, he advises Fletcher to seek out those who stand "in awe of Him they love—persons who are vigorously working out their salvation, persons athirst for full redemption."[36] These would "commonly be poor and mean," but, Wesley assures Fletcher, "if you converse with these humbly and simply an hour at a time, with prayer before and prayer after, you will not complain of the unprofitableness of conversation, or find any need of turning hermit."[37]

---

31. Wesley to Ann Bolton, June 28, 1784, 223–24.
32. Wesley to Harriet Lewis, April 2, 1789, 127.
33. Wesley to Harriet Lewis, April 2, 1789, 127.
34. Wesley to John Fletcher, March 20, 1768, 83.
35. Wesley to John Fletcher, March 20, 1768, 84.
36. Wesley to John Fletcher, March 20, 1768, 84.
37. Wesley to John Fletcher, March 20, 1768, 84.

This advice is not far removed from that he gives to John Robson: "As to lukewarm company, I can only advise you (1) to keep out of it—as much as you can; (2) when you cannot, to pray before, after, and during your stay in it fervently and without ceasing."[38] All of friendship, he felt, should be covered in prayer.

Love and marriage are central human concerns, and that applied to Wesley as well as to his friends. To Samuel Furly, seeking to extricate himself from a love affair, Wesley issues the sharp advice, "Never write to that person at all, nor of her; and continue instant in prayer."[39] To Ann Foard, who was about to be married, he advises, "You will do well likewise constantly to pray with as well as for one another."[40]

Marriage, Wesley thought, could potentially lead to the backsliding of serious believers. On the other hand, it provided an opportunity to mutually strengthen believers through unity in prayer. To Mrs. Barton and her new husband, he cautions, "Both of you have now more need than ever continually to watch and pray that you enter not into temptation. There will be a great danger of so cleaving to each other as to forget God, or of being so taken up with a creature as to abate your hunger and thirst after righteousness."[41] He advises Mrs. Cock, who had recently married, to pray for the sanctification of her husband. He assures her that "it was no sin to marry a child of God—yea, though he were but a babe in Christ."[42] He further encourages her in prayer, writing, "And surely, if you pray mightily for him, the Lord will hear your prayer, and supply whatever is yet wanting in his faith, till he is happy and holy and perfect in love."[43] Wesley's heart was for couples to grow in Christ, individually and together, through prayer.

These bits of advice, so cautious and hopeful, yet seldom wandering far from the central point of prayer, are a startling contrast to what Wesley wrote to his own gossiping and backbiting wife: "You cut yourself off from joint prayer. For how can I pray with one that is daily watching to do me hurt? You cut yourself off from all friendly intercourse with many who would otherwise rejoice to converse with and serve you. You rob yourself of many precious opportunities of public prayer and attending the Lord's

---

38. Wesley to John Robson, September 30, 1735, 183.
39. Wesley to Samuel Furly, February 21, 1756, 164.
40. Wesley to Ann Foard, December 2, 1767, 68.
41. Wesley to Mrs. Barton, April 9, 1769, 131.
42. Wesley to Mrs. Cock, April 7, 1789, 128.
43. Wesley to Mrs. Cock, April 7, 1789, 128.

Table."[44] In this, one can hear Wesley's heart yearning for the close spiritual fellowship of prayer with his wife, and the pain he felt in being unable to pray with her.

Unfortunately, many people desire close spiritual fellowship with their family members and cannot share that fellowship because their family members are unsaved. Wesley's faith in the power of prayer, however, was unshakable. He fully believed that one's prayers would lead directly to the salvation of unsaved family members. In a letter to Henry Eames, who was rejoicing in the "change wrought in several of [his] children,"[45] Wesley encourages him to keep praying: "You can have no reason to doubt but that He will give you your mother also if you continue earnest in prayer."[46] No doubt part of this was due to the testimony of his own brother Charles who writes to him about his own spiritual awakening: "I am not ashamed to desire your prayers. Tis owing in great measure to somebody's [prayers] (my mother's, most likely) that I am come to think as I do, for I can't tell myself how or when I first awoke out of my lethargy—only that it was not long after you went away."[47] John Wesley's advice to others to pray for spiritual awakenings in their family members underscores the importance he ascribed to this.

Likewise, Wesley used the same language of "giving" to speak of a family member coming into salvation through prayer when writing to Ann Loxdale: "You have, indeed, reason to rejoice over your sister. Is she not given you in answer to prayer? And have you not encouragement even from this very thing to expect that more of your family will be given you? Those are true words, when in His own strength you wrestle with God— 'My powerful groans Thou canst not bear, / Nor stand the violence of my prayer, / My prayer omnipotent.'"[48] Prayer, Wesley knew, was a powerful force for spiritual transformation in the lost.

Wesley was convinced that prayer could help persuade those about to make foolish decisions in love and marriage. He wrote to Mary Stokes regarding her friend, who was about to choose a husband who had "no liking either to the doctrine or discipline of the Methodists"[49] rather than

44. Wesley to Molly Wesley, November 24, 1759, 80.
45. Wesley to Henry Eames, July 15, 1789, 153.
46. Wesley to Henry Eames, July 15, 1789, 153–54.
47. Charles Wesley to John Wesley, January 5–22, 1729.
48. Wesley to Ann Loxdale, July 14, 1781, 73.
49. Wesley to Mary Stokes, January, 1772, 303.

a trusted Methodist preacher. Wesley says of her, in a letter to Ann Bolton, "It is only free, open love, however shy she may be, whereby you can make any impression upon her. And love, seconded with prayer, will prevail."[50] Wesley faced a similar situation with another woman: "What a proof we had the other day that He heareth the prayer. Arguments availed nothing with Rob. Howard's daughter. She was utterly resolved not to part with her idol, but to marry him next week. But after five minutes' prayer, her heart was changed and she determined 'to see him no more.' Who is so great a God as our God?"[51]

Opposition

Prayer was the first recourse of Wesley when facing human opposition, either personal or against his ministry. He writes to the lonely Mrs. Woodhouse, "He has permitted that difference which prevents your finding comfort even in a near relation, that you may seek it with a free and disengaged heart in him who will never deceive your hope.... The neglect of others should incite you to double diligence in private prayer."[52] To Richard Rodda, who was apparently experiencing opposition to his ministry, Wesley writes, "It is a good thing to stop Mr. Salmon; but it would be a far greater thing to reclaim him. And why should we suppose it to be impossible? Who knows the power of mighty prayer?"[53] Sometimes opposition degenerated into outright persecution.

Persecution was the issue when Adam Clarke and another Methodist preacher were assaulted by a group of men during their ministry. When the Court Royal refused to defend them, they wrote to Wesley for advice. When he responds, he again highlights the importance of prayer: "The main point seems to be to remove the prejudice of the Bailiff. If possible, this should be done by fair means. Law is the last and worst means, though it is sometimes necessary. But I should expect far more from prayer."[54] In the same vein, he advises Duncan McAllum, "I think it is by prayer that you must alter the

---

50. Wesley to Ann Bolton, December 28, 1771, 295.
51. Wesley to Robert Carr Brackenbury, July 9, 1781, 274.
52. Wesley to Mrs. Woodhouse, January 1, 1770, 174.
53. Wesley to Richard Rodda, January 17, 1787, 364.
54. Wesley to Adam Clarke, November 21, 1787, 23.

purpose of the Earl of Findlater."[55] In all of these situations, Wesley looked to prayer as the means to find victory.

Reconciliation

From time to time, Wesley found himself in heated arguments with those who mistrusted him and rejected his doctrine. If Wesley's argument did not convince his opponent, he frequently stopped arguing and suggested they pray together. Sometimes, a supernatural transformation occurred, and his former enemy reconciled with him, or at least changed his or her attitude. In 1739, Wesley visited Mrs. Compden of Oxford, who was "enraged" at what Wesley was teaching and was "zealous in opposing it."[56] In his journal, Wesley explains that, "finding argument to be of no other effect, than to inflame her more and more, I broke off the dispute, and desired we might join in prayer, which she so far consented to as to kneel down. In a few minutes she fell into an extreme agony, both of body and soul; and soon after cried out with the utmost earnestness, 'Now I know I am forgiven for Christ's sake.'"[57] Twenty years later, he met a woman who "warmly told" him she could not like his doctrine. "I desired we might pray. God quickly answered for himself: Her heart was broke in pieces. She was filled with love, and grief, and shame; but could only tell it by her eyes and her tears."[58] Wesley personally experienced the power of prayer in turning opposition to reconciliation.

Wesley was even more ready to abandon argumentation for prayer when disputing with his friends and those in Methodist societies who were generally predisposed to support him. Once again, he often found that praying together was a surer way forward than further arguing. In 1739, in his own society, division crept in after he was gone for a mere eight days. He records, "And when we met in the evening, instead of reviving the dispute, we all betook ourselves to prayer. Our Lord was with us. Our divisions were healed."[59] In 1741 in Pontypool, Wesley found that certain men had been among his clergy there and taken "true pains . . . to set them against my

---

55. Wesley to Duncan McAllum, January 20, 1789, 110.
56. Wesley, *Works* (Jackson) 1:175 (March 6, 1739).
57. Wesley, *Works* (Jackson) 1:175 (March 6, 1739).
58. Wesley, *Works* (Jackson) 2:513 (September 9, 1759).
59. Wesley, *Works* (Jackson) 1:205 (June 18, 1739).

brother and me."[60] However, "instead of disputing we betook ourselves to prayer; and all our hearts were knit together as at the first."[61] Less than a week later, he met with three men late at night. "They immediately fell upon their favourite subject; on which when we had disputed two hours, and were just where we were at first, I begged we might exchange controversy for prayer. We did so, and then parted in much love, about two in the morning."[62] Reconciliation, however, did not always happen, despite prayer.

One division that deeply grieved Wesley was in the society on Fetter Lane. The division happened as a result of Moravian influence on the members, especially Quietism. Wesley and the faithful members left, but desired reconciliation. In 1741, these faithful members met together "for prayer and humbling our souls before God, if haply he might show us his will concerning our re-union with our brethren of Fetter-Lane."[63] Unfortunately, "it was clear to all, even those who were before the most eagerly desirous of it, that the time was not come."[64] This was not only because they held onto the "erroneous doctrines" of the Moravians, but because "many of us had found so much guile in their words, that we could scarce tell what they really held, and what not."[65] Despite prayer, reconciliation was not achieved.

Since prayer was sometimes effective at reconciling enemies, and often friends, Wesley did not hesitate to recommend prayer when mediating between others. For instance, Wesley met with two women in Portarlington who were "deeply prejudiced against each other."[66] Bringing in a witness resulted in all three being angry. "I perceived there was no remedy but prayer. So a few of us wrestled with God for above two hours." The result was that "anger and revenge were vanished away and melted down into love."[67] In Mountmellick, "some of the most earnest persons in the society were deeply prejudiced against each other."[68] Wesley brought them together and "laboured much to remove that prejudice. I used both argument and

---

60. Wesley, *Works* (Jackson) 1:339 (October 3, 1741).
61. Wesley, *Works* (Jackson) 1:339 (October 3, 1741).
62. Wesley, *Works* (Jackson) 1:340 (October 9, 1741).
63. Wesley, *Works* (Jackson) 1:309 (May 6, 1741).
64. Wesley, *Works* (Jackson) 1:309 (May 6, 1741).
65. Wesley, *Works* (Jackson) 1:309 (May 6, 1741). See chapter 11 of this book for more information.
66. Wesley, *Works* (Jackson) 2:194 (June 23, 1750).
67. Wesley, *Works* (Jackson) 2:194 (June 23, 1750).
68. Wesley, *Works* (Jackson) 3:286 (June 26, 1767).

persuasion; but it was all in vain. Perceiving that reasoning profited nothing, we betook ourselves to prayer. On a sudden the mighty power of God broke in upon them. The angry ones on both sides burst into tears, and fell on each other's necks. All anger and prejudice vanished away, and they were as cordially united as ever."[69] Results like this kept Wesley confident in the power of prayer, even when sometimes reconciliation did not happen.

Conclusion

Community and prayer are closely woven in Wesley's theology and practice. Community is the context in which prayer often happens, in preaching services and prayer meetings, and love for those present shapes prayer away from merely enthusiastic forms to more appropriate and edifying forms. The family is an important environment for learning how to pray, and friendships and family can be both powerful aids to, or distractions from, prayer. When facing opposition in ministry, Wesley frequently abandoned argumentation for prayer, often with good results, and advised others to do the same. His goal was to reconcile people to their enemies, and he looked for this as the ultimate answer to his prayers when opposed. For Wesley, prayer served as the lifeblood of the spiritual community.

---

69. Wesley, *Works* (Jackson) 3:286 (June 26, 1767).

— 8 —

Prayer in Practice

THE PRACTICE OF PRAYER in the Christian life is fraught with questions and concerns such as what one should pray for, and in what manner—or how one deals with situations when praying is difficult. John Wesley addressed all of these issues and more in his writings. This chapter examines Wesley's views on what one should (and should not) pray for, how one should look to receive guidance in prayer, and the attitude and demeanor one should take in prayer. Next, the chapter looks at Wesley's understanding of how faith and sin affect prayer and the nature and importance of private prayer. Finally, it examines the issues surrounding how often one should pray, especially when prayer becomes difficult.

Topics for Prayer

Throughout his writings, Wesley encouraged prayer on all sorts of topics. Most especially, he encouraged prayer about any desire or concern which weighed on the mind of the believer. His directions on this are most clear in his comments on Phil 4:6, writing,

> *Be* anxiously *careful for nothing*—If men are not gentle towards you, yet neither on this, nor any other account, be careful, but pray. Carefulness and prayer cannot stand together. *In every thing*— Great and small; *let your requests be made known*—They who by a

preposterous shame or distrustful modesty, cover, stifle, or keep in their desires, as if they were either too small or too great, must be racked with care; from which they are entirely delivered, who pour them out with a free and filial confidence: *to God*—It is not always proper to disclose them to men.[1]

There is nothing believers should scruple against when considering what to bring to God in prayer, since God's concern and providence cover every aspect of the condition of the world. "His eye is ever open, and his hand stretched out to direct every the minutest circumstance."[2] One of Wesley's correspondents wrote to him regarding her fear that she was praying for her family out of natural affection alone, rather than pure spirituality, and he advises her in his letter, "The praying much for those we love much is doubtless the fruit of affection, but such an affection as is well pleasing to God and is wrought in us by His own Spirit. Therefore it is certain the intercession that flows from that affection is according to the will of God."[3] This had not always been the case. For some time in his early life, Wesley felt it was only proper to pray for "spiritual" concerns. Eventually, circumstances pushed him to change his view. "For many years I had a kind of scruple with regard to praying for temporal things. But three or four years ago I was thoroughly persuaded that scruple was unnecessary. Being then straitened much, I made it [a] matter of prayer; and I had an immediate answer. It is true we can only ask outward blessings with reserve, 'If this is best; if it be Thy will.' And in this manner we may certainly plead the promise, 'All these things shall be added to you.'"[4]

The sin "unto death," about which John the apostle told his readers not to pray, is interpreted by Wesley to be "total apostasy from both the power and form of godliness."[5] Although Wesley declares, "There is no man . . . that is wholly void of the grace of God," he adds the clarification, "unless he has quenched the Spirit."[6] Presumably, those who have so totally quenched the Spirit as to become apostate are beyond salvation, and prayer for them is

---

1. Wesley, *Explanatory Notes*, 513.
2. Wesley, "Sermon 23," 288.
3. Wesley to Miss March, June 17, 1774, 91.
4. Wesley to Mrs. Barton, November 5, 1770, 206. Wesley also suggested that it was useless to pray for deliverance from wandering thoughts that did not stem from or lead to sinful tempers. See the section "Difficult Prayer" later in this chapter.
5. Wesley, *Explanatory Notes*, 641.
6. Wesley, "Sermon 85," 512.

a pointless waste. However, Wesley also offers an additional interpretation of the "sin unto death;" he suggests that it might also mean a sin "which God has determined to punish with death."[7] In this case, then, if one has supernatural revelation regarding God's will in punishing a sin with death, the believer should not pray against God's revealed will.

Guidance

One popular request in believers' prayers was for guidance. Wesley was confident that those who sought God's guidance in prayer would not be easily led astray. "There is no danger of your taking any step that is materially wrong if you continue instant in prayer."[8] "Be much in prayer, and God will direct you right."[9] "I can only say, 'Give yourself to prayer; and then act, in the name and in the fear of God, as you are fully persuaded in your own mind.'"[10] In directing a Methodist society that was looking for a new meeting location, he counsels, "If you make it a matter of prayer, God will surely provide a better place for His service."[11]

The relationship between guidance through prayer and guidance through the advice of others, however, is a little ambiguous. Wesley, when considering whether the Methodists should separate from the Church of England, made the decision not to separate and defends the decision by pointing to the process: "We have done nothing rashly, nothing without deep and long consideration, hearing and weighing all objections, and much prayer."[12] However, on at least one other occasion, he advised a correspondent against seeking the advice of others, but going only to God in prayer: "May the God of wisdom direct you in all your steps! And I conceive He will rather do this by giving you light directly from Himself in meditation and private prayer than by the advice of others, who can hardly be impartial in so tender a point. Is it not, then, advisable that you should much commune with God and your own heart?"[13]

---

7. Wesley, *Explanatory Notes*, 641.
8. Wesley to Ann Loxdale, July 24, 1782, 131.
9. Wesley to Adam Clarke, July 2, 1786, 335.
10. Wesley to Sophia Cooke, June 20, 1786, 335.
11. Wesley to Joshua Keighley, February 19, 1787, 371.
12. Wesley to Thomas Adam, October 31, 1755, 150.
13. Wesley to James Lowther, July 1, 1759, 66.

In addition, Wesley experienced at least one situation where a believer refused to listen to others and persisted in a foolish course of action she felt clearly directed to in prayer. His sister had fallen in love with a man Wesley did not approve of, and his conversation with her availed nothing. Wesley recounts, "I talked with her about it; but she had 'so often made it matter of prayer that she could not be deceived.' In a week he dropped her, courted her elder sister, and as soon as was convenient married her."[14] In light of this situation, the advice Wesley gave emphasized neither advice from others nor guidance in prayer, but a third source—the word of God: "And you will be the better enabled by your own experience to guard all, especially young persons, from laying stress upon anything but the written Word of God. Guard them against reasoning in that dangerous manner, 'If I was deceived in this, then I was deceived in thinking myself justified.' Not at all; although nature, or Satan in the latter case, admirably well mimicked the works of God. By mighty prayer repel all those suggestions."[15]

Near the end of his life, Wesley reflected back in a letter on the nature of God's guidance, and in his writing expresses a balanced approach that was the fruit of years of experience guiding others and being guided himself: "A great man observes that there is a threefold leading of the Spirit: some He leads by giving them on every occasion apposite texts of Scripture; some by suggesting reasons for every step they take—the way by which He chiefly leads me; and some by impressions. But He judges the last to be the least desirable way, as it is often impossible to distinguish dark impressions from divine or even diabolical."[16]

Attitude in Prayer

Besides thanksgiving and faith, Wesley mentioned several other attitudes connected to proper prayer in his writings. Earnestness, or seriousness and sincerity, comes up multiple times. He enjoined believers to "let us earnestly pray."[17] Patience is also important. Wesley saw in the conception of John the Baptist not only God's answer to the patient waiting of Zechariah and Elizabeth, but also a model. He says, "Let us wait patiently for the Lord, and leave to his own wisdom the time and manner wherein he will

---

14. Wesley to Ann Bolton, August 31, 1784, 233.
15. Wesley to Ann Bolton, August 31, 1784, 233.
16. Wesley to Freeborn Garrettson, July 15, 1789, 154.
17. Wesley, *Explanatory Notes*, 62; see also 372.

appear for us."[18] Likewise, Wesley comments on the book of Philippians, "And joy peculiarly enlivens prayer. The sum of the whole epistle is, I rejoice. Rejoice ye."[19]

The two parables on prayer in Luke 18 furnish an opportunity for Wesley to point out the importance of persistence and humility in prayer: "This and the following parable warn us against two fatal extremes, with regard to prayer: the former against faintness and weariness, the latter against self confidence."[20] One form in which the Pharisees' self-confidence in prayer manifested itself was, in Wesley's eyes, the use of "too amorous" language in prayer and worship.

An unnamed person of "deep piety as well as judgment" once remarked to Wesley that some of Isaac Watts's hymns "were (as he phrased it) 'too *amorous*, and fitter to be addressed by a lover to his fellow-mortal, than by a sinner to the most high God.'"[21] Wesley writes that this criticism was applicable to another unnamed hymn writer as well: "Are [his hymns] not full of expressions which strongly savour of 'knowing Christ after the flesh?' yea, and in a more gross manner, than anything which was ever before published in the English tongue? What pity is it that those coarse expressions should appear in many truly spiritual hymns! How often, in the midst of excellent verses, are lines inserted which disgrace those that precede and follow!"[22]

Likewise, when translating some of the hymns of the Moravian Brethren, Wesley emphasizes that he took "sufficient care to pare off every improper word or expression,—every one that may seem to border on a familiarity which does not so well suit the mouth of a worm of the earth, when addressing himself to the God of heaven."[23] He took particular care "in all the hymns which are addressed to our blessed Lord, to avoid every *fondling* expression, and to speak as to the most High God; to him that is 'in glory equal with the Father, in majesty co-eternal.'"[24]

So strong was his aversion to "fondling expressions" that he refused to use the term "dear" in reference to the Almighty, in constructions such

---

18. Wesley, *Explanatory Notes*, 140.
19. Wesley, *Explanatory Notes*, 506.
20. Wesley, *Explanatory Notes*, 189.
21. Wesley, "Sermon 117," 293.
22. Wesley, "Sermon 117," 293.
23. Wesley, "Sermon 117," 293.
24. Wesley, "Sermon 117," 293.

as "dear Lord" or "dear Saviour." Although even his brother Charles Wesley disagreed with him on this, John Wesley defended his practice, saying, "Is not this using too much familiarity with the great Lord of heaven and earth? Is there any Scripture, any passage either in the Old or New Testament, which justifies this manner of speaking? Does any of the inspired writers make use of it, even in the poetical scriptures?"[25] He was certainly not comfortable with these sorts of expressions.

Wesley rejected the idea that losing these fondling terms would diminish true devotion to God. Rather, he said, it would "enliven the prayer that is properly addressed to Him, who, though he was very man, yet was very God."[26] On the other hand, the use of such terms, "this improper familiarity with God our Creator, our Redeemer, our Governor, is naturally productive of very evil fruits,"[27] the most important being that it dampened reverence to God.

Kenneth J. Collins sees Wesley's objection to these expressions as fitting into a larger pattern of Christology that leaned in a Monophysite direction, tending to deny the humanity of the incarnation rather than to take any chance of diminishing Christ's divinity. Collins concludes, however, that Wesley's Christology "is in line with orthodoxy, with the council of Chalcedon in particular (which offered the formula two natures in one person), even if there was some hesitancy on Wesley's part in his *genuine* affirmation of the human nature of Christ. . . . For Wesley, Christ is truly both God and human, though he tended, out of respect and honor, to emphasize the former."[28]

Formality

Despite many of his high church attitudes, Wesley considered formality, especially in prayer, as the enemy of true heart religion. His conviction is evident as he writes, with some heat, about empty formality in *A Farther Appeal to Men of Reason and Religion, Part III*: "Have not you substituted, in the place of the religion of the heart, something (I do not say equally sinful, but) equally vain, and foreign to the worshipping of God 'in spirit and in truth?' What else can be said even of prayer, (public or private,)

---

25. Wesley, "Sermon 117," 294.
26. Wesley, "Sermon 117," 295.
27. Wesley, "Sermon 117," 295.
28. Collins, *Theology*, 95.

in the manner wherein you generally perform it? as a thing of course, running round and round in the same dull track, without either the knowledge or love of God, without one heavenly temper, either attained or improved! O what mockery of God is this!"[29]

In the conference minutes of 1744, Wesley addresses two practical ways to prevent formality from creeping into prayer: "How shall we exclude formality from prayer and conversation? 1. By preaching frequently on that head. 2. By watching always, that we may only speak what we feel."[30] Decades later, still considering the same question, Wesley had come to the conclusion that one of the most effective means to oppose formality was through the experience of temptation; he says, "We had been speaking ... [of] the means of preventing spiritual religion from degenerating into formality. It is continually needful to guard against this, as it strikes at the root of the whole work of God. One means whereby God guards us against it is temptation, and indeed crosses of every kind. By these He keeps us from sleeping, as do others, and stirs us up to watch unto prayer."[31] As effective as preaching and watching might be, Wesley's own experience showed him that the threat of falling into sin set the righteous on guard against formality in a way that mere preaching and watching alone did not.

Faith and Sin

One important quality or attitude in prayer is faith. Faith is the firm belief that God will answer one's prayer. Wesley writes of such faith, "Pray, therefore, and look for the answer of your prayer. It shall come, and not tarry!"[32] Faith leads directly to boldness in prayer. "We shall grow in boldness the more, the more we use it; and it is by the same method, added to prayer, that we are to recover anything we have lost."[33] Faith in God's answer to one's prayer is a by-product of faith in the nature and character of God as loving and merciful. "Being greatly embarrassed by the necessities of the poor, we spread all our wants before God in solemn prayer; believing that he would sooner 'make windows in heaven' than suffer his

---

29. Wesley, *Farther Appeal, Part III*, 202.
30. Wesley, *Minutes of Conferences*, 25.
31. Wesley to Penelope Newman, August 9, 1776, 227.
32. Wesley to Philothea Briggs, August 14, 1771, 273.
33. Wesley to Mary Cooke, December 14, 1785, 304.

truth to fail."[34] Wesley believed that God was a God of mercy and truth, and he trusted that God to answer his prayers.

Faith and prayer have a mutually reinforcing dynamic in Wesley's theology. In a comment on John 15:7, he says, "Prayers themselves are a fruit of faith, and they produce more fruit."[35] Those who believe will pray, because they have confidence that their prayer will be heard. Wesley's comments on 1 John 5:14 are revealing: "*And we*—Who believe. Have this farther *confidence in him, that he heareth*—That is, favourably regards, whatever prayer we offer in faith, according to his revealed will."[36] Furthermore, "The consequence of your going and bearing fruit will be, that all your prayers will be heard."[37] This happens because "faith anticipates the blessings"[38] of an answer to prayer. Faith prepares the heart to receive the answer to prayer; "when the event comes, we know it comes in answer to our prayer."[39]

Those who pray, believe, because, as he said in writing to a correspondent, "Unbelief is either total, the absence of faith; or partial, the want of more faith. In the latter sense every believer may complain of unbelief, unless when he is filled with faith and the Holy Ghost. Then it is all midday. Yet even then we may pray, 'Lord, increase our faith.'"[40] Faith, then, is a product of prayer. Those who believe, will pray, and those who pray, believe.

The other side of faith is resignation. When one has faith that God is loving and merciful, and has heard one's prayer, one can leave the answer in the hands of God without anxiety. "He orders all things well; and being assured of this, we need be careful for nothing: it is enough that in all things we may make our requests with thanksgiving. I make no doubt but He will hear the prayers on behalf of your whole family; but the time and manner of answering our prayers He reserves in His own power."[41] Wesley looked to Christ's prayer in the garden of Gethsemane as a model for how to express faithful resignation in prayer, saying, "Various scriptures show that we may pray with resignation for the life or ease of a friend: it is enough that every petition be closed with, 'Not as I will, but

---

34. Wesley, *Works* (Jackson) 3:486 (December 31, 1772).
35. Wesley, *Explanatory Notes*, 258.
36. Wesley, *Explanatory Notes*, 640–41.
37. Wesley, *Explanatory Notes*, 259.
38. Wesley, *Explanatory Notes*, 641.
39. Wesley, *Explanatory Notes*, 641.
40. Wesley to Miss March, July 1, 1772, 326.
41. Wesley to Mrs. Johnston, June 1, 1778, 310–11.

as Thou wilt.'"[42] If Christ could pray with resignation, Wesley understood that Christians could do so as well.

Wesley believed that faith led to prayer, but he also believed that sin both inhibited prayer, and inhibited God's answering prayer. In response to the statement by James, "Ye ask not," Wesley comments, "And no marvel; for a man full of evil desire, of envy or hatred, cannot pray."[43] Paul's statement to Timothy that he wanted men to be "lifting up holy hands, without wrath and doubting," were to Wesley a sinful trifecta of what would inhibit God's answering prayer. He comments on it, "And wrath, or unholy actions, or want of faith in him we call upon, are the three grand hindrances of God's hearing our petitions. Christianity consists of faith and love, embracing truth and grace: therefore the sum of our wishes should be, to pray, and live, and die, without any wrath or doubt."[44] Elsewhere, he comments, "All sin hinders prayer; particularly anger. Anything at which we are angry is never more apt to come into our mind than when we are at prayer; and those who do not forgive will find no forgiveness from God."[45] To pray, and pray well, Wesley believed one must put aside sinful thoughts, attitudes, and actions.

Private Prayer

As a young man, Wesley was not initially a proponent or practitioner of private prayer. At least his diaries, which contained a punctilious account of how his hours were spent each day, did not record any entries of private prayer up through 1727. The next couple of years of his diaries were lost, but when they pick up again in 1729, private prayers appear several times a day. What happened specifically to cause Wesley to change his personal devotions so radically is unknown, but the time coincides with his service as a curate for his father in Epworth and Wroot.[46] The change was lasting, however. For the rest of his life, he called attention to the importance of private prayer.

In the 1745 minutes to the conference, Wesley describes the daily schedule of an assistant: "They may spend the mornings (from six to twelve)

42. Wesley to Miss March, August 12, 1769, 147.
43. Wesley, *Explanatory Notes*, 603.
44. Wesley, *Explanatory Notes*, 541.
45. Wesley, *Explanatory Notes*, 614.
46. Wesley, *Manuscript Prayer Manual*, ii.

in reading, writing, and prayer: from twelve to five, visit the sick and well: and from five to six use private prayer."[47] Some years later, he described the schedule for the children in the Kingswood School. After mentioning that the children rise at 4 a.m. and spend their first hour privately, he describes their devotional practice. This hour is spent "partly in reading, partly in singing, partly in self-examination or meditation, (if capable of it,) and partly in prayer" and that children "at first use a short form, (which is varied continually,) and then pray in their own words."[48] Private prayer was important for all Christians, from children to preachers.

In 1762, while rebuking the leadership of a society for descending into enthusiasm, Wesley writes, "I dislike your saying that one saved from sin . . . needs no self-examination, no times of private prayer; needs not mind little or outward things; and that he cannot be taught by any person who is not in the same state."[49] In the conference minutes of 1765, Wesley's solution to the problem of "superficial religion" was to "earnestly recommend private prayer, reading the Scriptures, and universal self-denial."[50] In the "Large" minutes of 1770–72, Wesley dealt with the question, "Why are we not more holy?" with a series of searching counter-questions, among which is, "Do you recommend the five-o'clock hour for private prayer? Do you observe it? Do not you find that any time is no time?"[51] Wesley understood that the neglect of private prayer was a key component of shallow or backslidden Christianity.

Relative Importance

For Wesley, the discipline of regular prayer was of utmost importance. "And private prayer you must never omit."[52] One should never neglect prayer, even for the work of the ministry. "Let not your works of mercy rob you of time for private prayer,"[53] he admonished. Nor did he, as a fellow of Oxford, think that schoolwork was a legitimate excuse for neglecting one's prayer life. "Let no study swallow up or entrench upon the hours of private

---

47. Wesley, *Minutes of Conferences*, 28.
48. Wesley, "Short Account of School," 285.
49. Wesley, *Works* (Jackson) 3:119–20 (October 29, 1762).
50. Wesley, *Minutes of Conferences*, 53.
51. Wesley, *Minutes of Conferences*, 524–25 ("Large" Minutes, 1763).
52. Wesley to Ann Taylor, March 8, 1787, 374.
53. Wesley to Ann Bolton, August 25, 1771, 275–76.

prayer. *Nil tanti*. ["Nothing is of such importance."] Simplify both religion and every part of learning as much as possible. Be all alive to God, and you will be useful to men!"[54] He even rejected public prayer as an acceptable substitute for private prayers: "Certainly your friend will suffer loss if he does not allow himself time every day for private prayer. Nothing will supply the want of this. Praying with others is quite another thing. Besides, it may expose us to great danger; it may turn prayer into an abomination to God: for 'Guilty we speak, if subtle from within / Blows on our words the self-admiring sin!'"[55] Prayer in public could tempt one to pride, and so was not a substitute for private prayer.

As important as prayer was, however, Wesley recognized that limits were necessary. To a young woman with a sensitive conscience, who was in danger of taking Wesley's words as law, he brought perspective: "It is a great thing to spend all our time to the glory of God. But you need not be scrupulous as to the precise time of reading and praying; I mean, as to dividing it between one and the other. A few minutes one way or the other are of no great importance."[56] He advised a woman suffering from a nervous disorder, "Sleep early: never sit up later than ten o'clock for any business whatever—no, not for reading or prayer; do not murder for sacrifice."[57] Wesley understood that even good things, taken to the extreme, ultimately became unhealthy. Although his main work was in awakening people to more fervent devotion, he always recognized that spiritual balance was a real thing, and he encouraged the devout to find that healthy balance.

Difficult Prayer

Charles Wesley wrote to his brother, John, concerning his experience in difficult prayer: "One who like me has for almost 13 years been utterly inattentive at public prayers can't expect to find there that warmth he has never known at his first seeking. He must knock oftener than once before tis opened to him, and is (I think) in some measure answerable for a heartlessness of which he himself is the cause."[58] Awakening his heart in prayer after many years being cold and inattentive was not the only thing that made

---

54. Wesley to Joseph Benson, November 30, 1770, 212.
55. Wesley to Miss March, June 27, 1760, 100-101.
56. Wesley to Miss March, March 4, 1760, 86.
57. Wesley to Mrs. Knapp, March 25, 1781, 52.
58. Charles Wesley to John Wesley, May 5, 1729, 97.

prayer difficult for Charles Wesley, however. In the very same letter, he also relates another situation: "An accident . . . has lately happened to me, which has made me resolve never upon any account to omit or defer my prayers."[59] Arriving home late one Saturday evening, he found himself "utterly averse to prayers and spent half an hour in vain in striving to recollect" his "dissipated thoughts."[60] He finally gave up, skipped his prayers, and went to bed. He "passed the whole night in the utmost trouble and discomposure of mind."[61] The next morning, he considered not receiving the sacrament, since he was "even without the least immediate preparation," but decided that it was probably a worse sin to "turn [his] back upon the sacrament."[62] The end result was that he "not only received the sacrament at that time with greater warmth than usual, but afterwards found [his] resolutions of pursuing considerably strengthened."[63] His faithfulness in receiving the sacrament led to receiving spiritual grace, despite his difficulty in praying.

Charles Wesley's experiences are a sample of the recurring pattern of difficulty in prayer that John Wesley addressed in his teaching and ministry. John Wesley's approach was to encourage persistence in prayer while assuring the one having difficulty that difficult prayer was still prayer and was still heard and answered by God. He writes, "It is certainly right to pray whether we can pray or no. God hears even when we hardly hear ourselves."[64] On another occasion, he advises, "Continue in private prayer, in spite of all coldness and wanderings, and you shall soon pray without ceasing."[65] Again, he wrote to a correspondent, "The most desirable prayer is that where we can quite pour out our soul and freely talk with God. But it is not this alone which is acceptable to Him. 'I love one,' said an holy man, 'that perseveres in dry duty.' Beware of thinking even this is labour lost. God does much work in the heart even at those seasons."[66] All prayer, even difficult prayer, is effective.

Persistence in prayer is important because spiritual growth is slow. Wesley explains, "At many times our advances in the race that is set before

---

59. Charles Wesley to John Wesley, May 5, 1729, 98.
60. Charles Wesley to John Wesley, May 5, 1729, 98.
61. Charles Wesley to John Wesley, May 5, 1729, 98.
62. Charles Wesley to John Wesley, May 5, 1729, 98.
63. Charles Wesley to John Wesley, May 5, 1729, 99.
64. Wesley to Mary Bosanquet, March 26, 1770, 187.
65. Wesley to Damaris Perronet, March 30, 1771, 235.
66. Wesley to Miss March, June 25, 1771, 262.

us are clear and perceptible; at other times they are no more perceptible (at least to ourselves) than the growth of a tree."[67] He continues by pointing out that the Christian's source of strength for persistent prayer is faith in the grace of God to complete his work in the individual: "At any time you may pray—'Strength and comfort from Thy word / Imperceptibly supply.' And when you perceive nothing, it does not follow that the work of God stands still in your soul; especially while your desire is unto Him, and while you choose Him for your portion. He does not leave you to yourself, though it may seem so to your apprehension."[68] In short, "nature and the devil will always oppose private prayer; but it is worthwhile to break through. That it is a cross will not hinder its being a blessing—nay, often the more reluctance the greater blessing."[69] Prayer, even difficult prayer, is a key component of spiritual growth, even when such growth is slow.

One particularly daunting aspect of difficult prayer is wandering thoughts. In August of 1731, he wrote to Mrs. Mary Pendarves about a friend of hers with a tender conscience who was distressed by some spiritual issues. "Two things she seems to complain of most," he says, "inattention in prayer and uneasiness before the sacrament. The latter probably is owing in good part to the former."[70] To clarify the situation, he posed two major questions for this friend of Mrs. Pendarves. The first major question about wandering thoughts was, "Can you help it?"[71] If the answer was negative, he posed a follow-up question: "Do you think God is good?" If the answer to this follow-up question was yes, then God "can't be displeased at what you can't avoid. That would be to be angry at Himself, since 'tis His will, not yours, that you are not more attentive."[72] The second major question was, "Do you expect while upon earth to be 'as the angels of God in heaven'? If not, you must expect to have a share in that infirmity which no one quite shakes off till he leaves earth behind him."[73] If all this sounds like a long way of saying what could simply be said, "You'll never get rid of wandering thoughts," Wesley does add some advice for how to gain a measure of victory over them: "Are you inattentive in prayer? pray oftener. Do you address to God twice a day

---

67. Wesley to Philothea Briggs, July 23, 1772, 331.
68. Wesley to Philothea Briggs, July 23, 1772, 331.
69. Wesley to Dorothy Furly, September 25, 1757, 229.
70. Wesley to Mrs. Pendarves, August 12, 1731, 102.
71. Wesley to Mrs. Pendarves, August 12, 1731, 102.
72. Wesley to Mrs. Pendarves, August 12, 1731, 102.
73. Wesley to Mrs. Pendarves, August 12, 1731, 102.

already? then do so three times. Do you find yourself very uneasy before the sacrament, though you receive it every month? your next resolution, with God's leave, should be to receive it every week."[74]

Two months later, Wesley wrote to Ann Granville about a friend of hers whose situation so much resembled the previous one that Wesley "had been in some doubt whether you did not speak of the same person."[75] At any rate, he concludes, "Neither do I believe that she will ever be wholly freed either from wandering thoughts in prayer. . . . I never heard or read of more than one living person (Mr. De Renty) who had quite shook off this weight."[76] Wesley saw that, in most cases, wandering thoughts were a normal part of being human.

The issue of wandering thoughts was so important, however, that Wesley devoted an entire sermon to it: "Sermon 41—Wandering Thoughts." This sermon is divided into four sections. In the first section, Wesley presented two different types of wandering thoughts: thoughts that wander from God and thoughts that wander "from the particular point we have in hand."[77] Each of these types has a different source. The former type originates in "sinful tempers,"[78] but the latter in human frailty and demonic distraction. Human frailty is not limited to disease or sickness, but "let a man be ever so healthy, he will be more or less delirious every four-and-twenty hours. For does he not sleep?"[79] Demons "harass and perplex us, and, so far as God permits, interrupt our thoughts, particularly when they are engaged on the best subjects."[80]

These two types of thoughts also fall into two classes: sinful and nonsinful. Sinful thoughts are those which either are produced by or lead to sinful tempers. Random thoughts, however, are not sinful, even if they are injected into one's mind by demons. Wesley conceded that demonically injected thoughts are "troublesome, and in that sense evil; but they are not sinful."[81] He argued that when the devil spoke to the Jesus, the Lord "doubtless

---

74. Wesley to Mrs. Pendarves, August 12, 1731, 102.
75. Wesley to Ann Granville, October 3, 1731, 317.
76. Wesley to Ann Granville, October 3, 1731, 319.
77. Wesley, "Sermon 41," 24.
78. Wesley, "Sermon 41," 25.
79. Wesley, "Sermon 41," 26.
80. Wesley, "Sermon 41," 27.
81. Wesley, "Sermon 41," 29.

understood what he said. He had therefore a thought correspondent to those words. But was it a sinful thought? We know it was not."[82]

Finally, one is delivered from these two types of wandering thoughts by two different types of deliverance. From the first type of thoughts, the sinful thoughts that wander from God, one is delivered through sanctification, for "every one that is perfected in love is unquestionably delivered."[83] On the other hand, the deliverance from the second type of thoughts is "widely different."[84] Wesley argued that as long as the causes remain, then the effects must also remain. As long as one is in a mortal human body, one is subject to the thoughts being "disturbed, broken, or interrupted, by any defect of the apprehension, judgment, or imagination, flowing from the natural constitution of the body."[85] And as long as one is in the world, one is subject to "those wandering thoughts which are occasioned by what we see and hear, among those by whom we are now surrounded."[86] Likewise, "as long as evil spirits roam to and fro in a miserable, disordered world, so long they will assault (whether they can prevail or no) every inhabitant of flesh and blood."[87] As none of these things will happen until "that which is immortal is come,"[88] Wesley advised that, instead of praying for deliverance from wandering thoughts, one should instead pray that all these "things may work together for our good."[89]

Fervency and Frequency

John Wesley's sister Martha Wesley quotes him in one of her letters: "If . . . 'God sees I sincerely desire devotion in prayer, and that I can do no more than desire it, why does not he do the rest?'"[90] The question, as Martha Wesley points out in her letter, is unanswerable this side of eternity. However, the assumption the question rests on, that one "can do no more than desire it," does not seem to be one that he continued to hold. In fact, Wesley repeatedly

---

82. Wesley, "Sermon 41," 29.
83. Wesley, "Sermon 41," 30.
84. Wesley, "Sermon 41," 30.
85. Wesley, "Sermon 41," 30.
86. Wesley, "Sermon 41," 31.
87. Wesley, "Sermon 41," 31.
88. Wesley, "Sermon 41," 31.
89. Wesley, "Sermon 41," 31.
90. Martha Wesley to John Wesley, January 10, 1730, 107.

urged others to pray fervently, and to believe that his urging was not vain. He asks, "Should you not earnestly strive and pray against thinking highly of your own understanding, or attainments in religion?"[91] Near the end of his life, he writes, "O stir up the gift of God that is in you, and wrestle with God in mighty prayer."[92] Nevertheless, he was still acutely aware of his own failures, as his question to Martha Wesley implies: "Sometimes I cannot accomplish the good I am employed in, because I do not pray more, and more fervently; and sometimes, even when I do pray, and that instantly, because I am not worthy that my prayer should be heard."[93] Lack of frequency and fervency is a barrier to answered prayer.

If one has problems with achieving fervency of devotion in prayer, one can at least increase the frequency of prayer. On this issue, Wesley counsels a lady by letter, advising that "she should add to the length of her prayers, or to the frequency of them."[94] A standard piece of advice, which he gives in correspondence, is to "rise at six and ... give the first hour of the day to your private and part of the next to your public addresses to God."[95] At the very least, he advises his bands "to use private prayer every day, and family prayer if you are the head of a family."[96] One of his personal resolutions, which he records at the beginning of every diary was, "To pray every hour, seriously, deliberately, fervently."[97] Even if he failed to meet this ideal perfectly, he regularly spent an hour in the mornings for prayer. For instance, on the ship to Georgia in 1735, he and his friends rose at 4 a.m. for an hour of private prayer.[98]

Spiritual Warfare

In a letter, George Whitefield urges Wesley to "wrestle, wrestle, honored sir, in prayer."[99] No doubt this advice was well-received by Wesley, as he often urged others with the same advice. One of the reasons frequency and fervency of prayer were so important to Wesley was his conviction that Christians

---

91. Wesley, *Works* (Jackson) 3:369 (June 27, 1769).
92. Wesley to William Black, March, 1790, 204.
93. Wesley to His Father, December 10, 1734, 173.
94. Pendarves to John Wesley, August 26, 1731, 33.
95. Wesley to Ann Granville, September 27, 1730, 55.
96. Willis to John Wesley, November 13, 1744, 193.
97. Wesley, "Manuscript Diaries Editorial Note," 431.
98. Wesley, *Works* (Jackson) 1:18 (October 21, 1735).
99. Whitefield to John Wesley, July 2, 1739, 133.

struggle against the forces of supernatural evil; as he says, "I afterwards exhorted our society . . . to 'pray always,' that they might not faint in their minds, though they were 'wrestling not against flesh and blood, but against principalities, and powers, and spiritual wickedness in high places.'"[100] In this struggle, prayer is one of the most important weapons; so important that Satan will do what he can to stop the Christian from praying. Wesley writes to a friend, "If that sickness you mention came (as is the case with some) only at the time of private prayer, I should incline to think it was preternatural, an angel of Satan permitted to buffet you."[101] Prayer can do things other, more human, weapons cannot. "Do not reason with the devil, but pray, wrestle with God, and He will give you light."[102] When advising Adam Clarke against facing "the prince of this world," Wesley says, "But if you continue instant in prayer God will put the bridle in his mouth."[103] To a correspondent who experienced a cloud of doubt spreading over her mind, Wesley writes, "You did right to pray, as you could pray; and this is the best method which can be taken in heaviness or darkness of any kind. Then, if sin be the cause, it will be discovered. But take care that you do not refuse any help; even rough speakers may be of service. Only spread what they say before the Lord, and He will turn it to good."[104] Prayer is a powerful weapon of spiritual warfare.

Conclusion

For many of the issues regarding the practice of prayer, Wesley had a firm stance. He believed one should pray about nearly anything and that God would give guidance in prayer; however, prayer for guidance should be balanced by wise counsel and the word of God, and one should take a reverent, but not overly formal, attitude in prayer. He believed private prayer was an important, but not the most important, part of one's spiritual life, and he encouraged believers to persevere when praying was difficult. He himself rose early to pray and prayed throughout the day and encouraged those around him to do the same. Praying was sometimes difficult because of the reality of the supernatural world, and supernatural opposition to prayer was to be expected.

100. Wesley, *Works* (Jackson) 1:273 (June 1, 1740).
101. Wesley to Ann Loxdale, July 14, 1781, 73.
102. Wesley to William Orpe, November 13, 1765, 315.
103. Wesley to Adam Clarke, November 9, 1787, 22.
104. Wesley to Dorothy Furly, October 21, 1757, 230–31.

— 9 —

Prayer and Supernatural Manifestations

As indicated at the end of the previous chapter, John Wesley took the supernatural seriously when thinking about prayer. This chapter explores that topic more deeply, first by addressing an early incident in his family's history that they considered supernatural, then by examining Wesley's theology of miracles, tongues, and healing in relation to prayer. Finally, it looks at some of Wesley's experiences praying for people who appeared to be afflicted with demons.

"Old Jeffries"

As a child, Wesley was sent away, like his elder brother, to boarding school. While he was gone, his family had some strange, apparently supernatural, experiences involving what they decided was a poltergeist. They nicknamed it "Old Jeffries" and believed that it haunted their Epworth rectory. From December 1716 until the end of January 1717,[1] the poltergeist disturbed the household primarily through its noisemaking, knocking, and drumming.

The specter seemed to give unusual attention to the prayers of the family. John Wesley's mother, Susanna Wesley, "was convinced it was preternatural, and earnestly prayed it might not disturb her in her own chamber,

---

1. Clarke, *Memoirs*, 212.

at the hours of retirement. And it never did."[2] The hours of retirement were the time she had her personal devotions, between 5 and 6 p.m.[3]

However, it regularly disturbed the family prayers, and at a quite specific time: "When he [Samuel Wesley, John Wesley's father] began the prayer for the king, a knocking began all round the room; and a thundering knock attended the amen. The same was heard from this time every morning and evening, while the prayer for the king was repeated."[4] Samuel Wesley tried an experiment. He writes, "On Friday the 25th, having prayers at church, I shortened, as usual, those in the family at morning, omitting the confession, absolution, and prayers for the king and prince. I observed when this is done, there is no knocking. I therefore used them one morning for a trial; at the name of king George, it began to knock, and did the same when I prayed for the prince."[5]

The political element to the timing of the poltergeist's interruptions was quite apparent, and some of the family members took to calling it a Jacobite.[6] While modern readers may find the idea of a poltergeist being so concerned with the prosaic mundanity of politics quaint, even naïve, certain elements must be taken into consideration. Jacobitism was a very real political threat to the stability of the country at the time, and eventually resulted in the Jacobite heir, "Bonnie" Prince Charles, leading an armed uprising in 1745. Moreover, for a Protestant nation, Jacobitism presented the threat of a return to power of Roman Catholicism and the persecution that would presumably entail. Finally, for those who believed in the divine right of kings, claims of kingship had the status of doctrinal disputes, and were thus inherently spiritual matters in which spiritual beings could be expected to take an interest.[7] Prayer for the king in this context was not a meaningless

2. Clarke, *Memoirs*, 209.
3. Clarke, *Memoirs*, 232.
4. Clarke, *Memoirs*, 209.
5. Clarke, *Memoirs*, 206.
6. Clarke, *Memoirs*, 205. In the Glorious Revolution of 1688, William of Orange, the Dutch nephew and son-in-law of James II, invaded England with the support of English military allies. As he approached London, most of the royal army deserted, and James II abandoned the throne and fled into exile. As he never formally renounced his claim to the throne, loyalists long awaited the return of the Jacobite heir to the throne.
7. In her private journal, Susanna Wesley clearly showed that she held to the divine right of kings: "Whether they did well in driving a prince from his hereditary throne, I leave to their own consciences to determine—though I cannot tell how to think that a king of England can ever be accountable to his subjects for any maladministrations or abuse of power, but, as he derives his power from God, so to him only he must answer for

convention, or even a mere political statement, but a spiritual act with spiritual consequences. John Wesley himself ascribed the presence of the spirit to an argument his parents had had over political elements in prayer: "The year before King William died, my father observed my mother did not say Amen to the prayer for the king. She said she could not; for she did not believe the prince of Orange was king. He vowed he would never cohabit with her till she did. He then took his horse and rode away; nor did she hear anything of him for a twelvemonth. He then came back, and lived with her as before. But I fear his vow was not forgotten before God."[8]

First, it should be pointed out that the account John Wesley gave of his father's vow is a little softer than the one his mother Susanna Wesley gave in private correspondence to her friend and confidant Lady Yarborough:

> 'Tis but a little while since he one evening observed in our Family prayers I did not say Amen to his prayer for K[ing] W[illiam] as I usually do to all others; upon which he retired to his study, and calling me to him asked me the reason of my not saying Amen to the Prayer. I was a little surprised at the question and don't well know what I answered, but too too well I remember what followed: He immediately kneeled down and imprecated the divine Vengeance upon himself and all his posterity if ever he touched me more or came into a bed with me before I had begged God's pardon and his, for not saying Amen to the prayer for the K[in]g.[9]

Although it is possible John Wesley was not privy to the details, the fact that the vow came to his mind as an explanation for the haunting implies that he certainly knew more than he let on in his explanation.

Furthermore, in offering this explanation, John Wesley tacitly accepted his family's conclusion that the events they experienced were supernatural in origin. However, the explanation he offered is different from the prior one proposed by his sister Emilia Wesley: "If you would know my opinion of the reason of this, I shall briefly tell you. I believe it to be witchcraft, for these reasons. About a year since, there was a disturbance at a town near us, that was undoubtedly witches; and if so near, why may they not reach us? Then my father had for several Sundays before its coming, preached

---

his using it." Susanna Wesley, *Complete Writings*, 204.

8. Clarke, *Memoirs*, 209.

9. Susanna Wesley, *Complete Writings*, 35.

warmly against consulting those that are called cunning men, which our people are given to; and it had a particular spite at my father."[10]

For Emilia Wesley, the disturbances were persecution by humans using supernatural means, in retaliation for her father's sermons. John Wesley, although no disbeliever in witches or witchcraft (see below), rather saw God's hand behind the events, and understood it ultimately as divine retribution for a rash and foolish vow.

John Wesley was away at boarding school when these supernatural events occurred, and he never experienced Old Jeffries himself. Nevertheless, he never disavowed these experiences later in life. In his mid-sixties, he argued that the prevalent attitude of dismissing reported paranormal events was not an evidence of intelligent discernment, but an artifact of an anti-supernatural bias in one's worldview:

> It is true, likewise, that the English in general, and indeed, most of the men of learning in Europe, have given up all accounts of witches and apparitions, as mere old wives' fables. I am sorry for it; and I willingly take this opportunity of entering my solemn protest against this violent compliment which so many that believe the Bible pay to those who do not believe it. I owe them no such service. I take knowledge, that these are at the bottom of the outcry which has been raised, and with such insolence spread throughout the nation, in direct opposition not only to the Bible but to the suffrage of the wisest and the best of men in all ages and nations. They well know, (whether Christians know it, or not,) that the giving up of witchcraft is, in effect, giving up the Bible; and they know, on the other hand, that if but one account of the intercourse of men with separate spirits be admitted, their whole castle in the air (Deism, Atheism, Materialism) falls to the ground. I know no reason, therefore, why we should suffer even this weapon to be wrested out of our hands. Indeed, there are numerous arguments besides, which abundantly confute their vain imaginations.[11]

Prayer and Miracles

Would Wesley expect a miraculous answer to prayer? The simple answer is "Absolutely," although any more complex answer must qualify and nuance that statement. On the one hand, he seems to have believed in the cessation

10. Clarke, *Memoirs*, 222.
11. Wesley, *Works* (Jackson) 3:324–25 (May 25, 1768).

of the supernatural gifts of the Spirit in the church. In his sermon "A Caution against Bigotry" he considered the applicability of Mark 9:38–39 to the Christians of his era, asking, rhetorically, "What is this to us, seeing no man now *casts out devils*? Has not the power of doing this been withdrawn from the Church, for twelve or fourteen hundred years?"[12] In his sermon "The More Excellent Way" he says, "It does not appear that these extraordinary gifts of the Holy Ghost were common in the Church for more than two or three centuries," and that after Constantine, "they almost totally ceased."[13]

However, these passages do not tell the whole story. First, Wesley understood that God was certainly free to act according to his will, and not to abide by any so-called natural laws. In his sermon "On Divine Providence," he quotes Alexander Pope's famous lines from *An Essay on Man*, "The Universal Cause / Acts not by partial, but by general laws,"[14] and rejects it outright, saying, "Admitting then, that, in the common course of nature, God does act by general laws, he has never precluded himself from making exceptions to them, whensoever he pleases; either by suspending that law in favour of those that love him, or by employing his mighty angels: By either of which means he can deliver out of all danger them that trust in him. 'What! You expect miracles, then?' Certainly I do, if I believe the Bible: For the Bible teaches me, that God hears and answers prayer: But every answer to prayer is, properly, a miracle."[15]

Wesley's argument here is that even "ordinary" answers to prayer have a supernatural origin in the response of God, contrary to the doctrines of the Deists.[16] Once one accepts that God acts within the realm of nature, there is no grounds to reject "extraordinary" answers to prayer, either. From this passage, it is clear that Wesley not only allows God sovereign freedom to act in a way that humans describe as "miraculous," but also that God does so in answer to prayer. This is supported in his commentary on other scriptural passages; for instance, the prayer offered in faith described in James 5:15 Wesley understood as saving the sick man "from his sickness," not just his sin, although "if any sin be the occasion of his

---

12. Wesley, "Sermon 38," 479.
13. Wesley, "Sermon 89," 26–27.
14. Wesley, "Sermon 67," 321.
15. Wesley, "Sermon 67," 322.
16. For John Wesley's foremost response to the Deist rejection of miracles in the early church up through the third century, see his "Letter to the Reverend Doctor Conyers Middleton Occasioned by His Late 'Free Inquiry,'" in *Works* (Jackson) 10:1–79.

sickness, it shall be forgiven him."[17] Likewise, Wesley quotes approvingly an "eminent author" in his comments on Mark 16:17, who said, "It was not one faith by which St. Paul was saved, another by which he wrought miracles. Even at this day in every believer faith has a latent miraculous power; (every effect of prayer being really miraculous;) although in many, both because of their own littleness of faith, and because the world is unworthy, that power is not exerted. Miracles, in the beginning, were helps to faith; now also they are the object of it."[18]

In fact, this idea, that lack of faith is the cause of lack of miracles (and not the divine withdrawing action of God) is also found in the contexts of the passages on cessation of the charismata, mentioned above. He explains the cause of the cessation of the charismata not as being "because there was no more occasion for them," but because "'the love of many,' almost of all Christians, so called, was 'waxed cold.'"[19] He continues, "This was the real cause why the extraordinary gifts of the Holy Ghost were no longer to be found in the Christian church; because the Christians were turned Heathens again, and had only a dead form left."[20] His explanation of this was clear enough that his editor, Albert Outler, comments, "An interesting note here that the possibility of 'the extraordinary gifts of the Holy Ghost' stands open, in principle, in any age of the church."[21] This is further supported by his comments on the "gifts of healing" mentioned in 1 Cor 12:9:

> The gift of healing need not be wholly confined to the healing diseases with a word or a touch. It may exert itself also, though in a lower degree, where natural remedies are applied; and it may often be this, not superior skill, which makes some physicians more successful than others. And thus it may be with regard to other gifts likewise. As, after the golden shields were lost, the king of Judah put brazen in their place, so, after the pure gifts were lost, the power of God exerts itself in a more covert manner, under human studies and helps; and that the more plentifully, according as there is the more room given for it.[22]

---

17. Wesley, *Explanatory Notes*, 606.
18. Wesley, *Explanatory Notes*, 136.
19. Wesley, "Sermon 89," 27.
20. Wesley, "Sermon 89," 27.
21. Outler in Wesley, *Works* (Bicentennial) 3:264n7.
22. Wesley, *Explanatory Notes*, 434.

This passage not only seems to suggest the "possibility" that "the extraordinary gifts of the Holy Ghost" might still be standing open, but, again, that God's miraculous gifts were never withdrawn by God. The miraculous use of them was only lost by the folly and unbelief of humanity; these gifts function still among God's people in as miraculous a way as believers give "room" for them with faith and holiness.[23]

Praying for the Weather

One topic on which Wesley prayed, and expected to be answered, was that of weather. In 1759, he was preaching under a hot sun. He writes, "The congregation was now larger by one half; but the sun was so scorching hot upon my head, that I was scarce able to speak. I paused a little, and desired God would provide us a covering, if it was for his glory. In a moment it was done; a cloud covered the sun, which troubled us no more."[24]

This attitude is especially evident in his sea voyages. He recounts that a storm that occurred when he was at sea was so bad they had to take in the sails. "But does not God hear the prayer? Mr. Hopper and I believed it our duty to make the trial again; and in a very few moments the wind was small, the sea fell, and the clouds dispersed; so we put up a little sail, and went on quietly and slowly, till the morning dawned."[25] In another instance, he was preparing to sail across the Irish Sea. "After sermon, I prayed that God would give us a full and speedy passage. While I was speaking, the wind sprung up; and in twelve hours brought us to Dublin Bay. Does not our Lord still hear the prayer?"[26]

A couple of years later, in 1787, Wesley had several answers to prayer on sea voyages. When their ship was stuck on a rock, he says, "We immediately went to prayer; and presently the ship, I know not how, shot off the rock, and pursued her way, without any more damage, than the

---

23. In this, Wesley was (knowingly or unknowingly) following the practical cessationism of John Calvin, who wrote that "the Lord is indeed present with his people in every age; and he heals their weaknesses as often as necessary, no less than of old; still he does not put forth these manifest powers, nor dispense miracles through the apostles' hands. For that was a temporary gift, and also quickly perished partly on account of men's ungratefulness." Calvin, *Institutes of the Christian Religion*, 1467.

24. Wesley, *Works* (Jackson) 2:492 (July 2, 1759).

25. Wesley, *Works* (Jackson) 2:201–2 (July 23, 1750).

26. Wesley, *Works* (Jackson) 4:300 (April 10, 1785).

wounding a few of her outside planks."[27] One month later, when Wesley and his companions "were in the middle of the rocks, with the sea rippling all round us, the wind totally failed. Had this continued, we must have struck upon one or other of the rocks: So we went to prayer, and the wind sprang up instantly."[28] A few weeks after that, they "had but just entered the ship when the wind died away. We cried to God for help, and it presently sprung up, exactly fair, and did not cease till it brought us into Penzance Bay."[29] Adam Clarke's comment on Wesley's praying in this instance neatly summarizes Wesley's faith-filled approach to prayer in general: "He expected to be heard, and he was heard."[30]

Praying in Tongues

Wesley gave a succinct summary of his understanding of praying in tongues in his commentary on 1 Cor 14:27: "It seems, the gift of tongues was an instantaneous knowledge of a tongue till then unknown, which he that received it could afterwards speak when he thought fit, without any new miracle."[31] While helpful, this is nevertheless ambiguous on some points currently controversial in the broader Christian world. Fortunately, Wesley made many revealing comments in his *Notes* on 1 Cor 12–14. From these comments, it is clear that Wesley considered speaking in tongues to be a miraculous gift, actuated by the Holy Spirit, of speaking in a human tongue for edification in prayer, or for the edification of the larger, local Christian community, when used in conjunction with interpretation of tongues, a separate gift.

First, speaking in tongues is a miraculous gift. In his comment on the phrase "Unless ye utter by the tongue" in 1 Cor 14:9, he says, "Which is miraculously given you."[32] Second, it is actuated by the Holy Spirit. He explains the phrase "speaking by the Spirit of God" in 1 Cor 12:3 by saying, "Is actuated by that Spirit, so as to speak with tongues, heal diseases, or cast out devils."[33]

27. Wesley, *Works* (Jackson) 4:387 (July 11, 1787).
28. Wesley, *Works* (Jackson) 4:392 (August 14, 1787).
29. Wesley, *Works* (Jackson) 4:398 (September 4, 1787).
30. Clarke in John Wesley, *Works* (Bicentennial) 24:57n64.
31. Wesley, *Explanatory Notes*, 439.
32. Wesley, *Explanatory Notes*, 438.
33. Wesley, *Explanatory Notes*, 433.

Although some have taken Paul's comment in 1 Cor 13:1, "Though I speak with the tongues of men and of angels," as implying that some operations of the gift of tongues involve speaking in angelic languages, this does not appear to be Wesley's understanding. His comment on the phrase "Though I speak with all the tongues" is "Which are upon earth, and with the eloquence of an angel."[34] Likewise, his comment on Paul's statement later in the chapter that "whether there be tongues, they shall cease" is "One language shall prevail among all the inhabitants of heaven, and the low and imperfect languages of earth be forgotten."[35]

Nor does Wesley understand the gift of tongues as primarily about supernaturally speaking a foreign language for missions or evangelism. Instead, following Paul's lead in 1 Cor 14, he understood it to be primarily for prayer and personal edification. He commented on Paul's statement that the one speaking in tongues "speaks, in effect, not to men, but to God" with "Who alone understands him."[36] When Paul considers the question of praying in an unknown tongue in verse 14, Wesley says, "*My spirit prayeth*—by the power of the Spirit I understand the words myself, *but my understanding is unfruitful*—The knowledge I have is no benefit to others."[37] On the next verse, he comments, "I will use my own understanding, as well as the power of the Spirit. I will not act so absurdly, as to utter in a congregation what can edify none but myself."[38] Finally, in verse 28, Wesley understands the phrase "Let him speak" as meaning "that tongue, if he find it profitable to himself in his private devotions."[39] None of these situations anticipates listeners who understand the speech in their own tongue. Even in Acts 2, Wesley sees the gift as symbolic rather than practical: "The miracle was not in the ears of the hearers, (as some have unaccountably supposed,) but in the mouth of the speakers. And this family praising God together, with the tongues of all the world, was an earnest that the whole world should in due time praise God in their various tongues."[40]

In his comment on Paul's command that those who speak in tongues should pray that they may interpret, Wesley identifies interpretation as "a

---

34. Wesley, *Explanatory Notes*, 435.
35. Wesley, *Explanatory Notes*, 436.
36. Wesley, *Explanatory Notes*, 437.
37. Wesley, *Explanatory Notes*, 438.
38. Wesley, *Explanatory Notes*, 438.
39. Wesley, *Explanatory Notes*, 439.
40. Wesley, *Explanatory Notes*, 277.

distinct gift."[41] A few verses later, when Paul is addressing the use of tongues in a public venue and says, "And let one interpret," Wesley comments, "Either himself, 1 Cor 14:13; or, if he have not the gift, some other, into the vulgar tongue."[42] Wesley's recognition that speaking and interpreting tongues are separate gifts argues that he did not consider the gift of tongues to be a supernaturally acquired knowledge of a foreign language, naturally employed, despite his comment that "he that received [the gift of tongues] could afterwards speak when he thought fit, without any new miracle."[43]

Prayer for Healing

Wesley had a great interest in medicine, and published a book of medicinal remedies, the *Primitive Physic*,[44] which went through twenty-four editions during his lifetime. Although he had a great respect for "natural" cures, he also believed—and prayed for—supernatural cures as well. Once, he had pain in his teeth, and as he writes, "I prayed with submission to the will of God. My pain ceased, and returned no more."[45] When his brother Charles Wesley was sick and unable to sleep, John Wesley and his friends prayed for him: "I went down to our brethren below, and we made our request known to God. When I went up again, he was in a sound sleep, which continued till the morning."[46] Another time, a man "lay in a high fever, almost dead for want of sleep. This was prevented by the violent pain in one of his feet, which was much swelled, and so sore, it could not be touched. We joined in prayer that God would fulfil his word, and give his beloved sleep. Presently the swelling, the soreness, the pain, were gone; and he had a good night's rest."[47]

Wesley did not limit his healing prayers to humans. As he spent most of his adult life on horseback or in a chaise, traveling from city to city preaching, his horses were an important part of his ministry. He was in a difficult situation when "one of the chaise-horses was on a sudden so lame, that he could hardly set his foot to the ground. It being impossible to procure any

41. Wesley, *Explanatory Notes*, 438.
42. Wesley, *Explanatory Notes*, 439.
43. Wesley, *Explanatory Notes*, 439.
44. Wesley, *Works* (Bicentennial) 32:97–266.
45. Wesley, *Works* (Jackson) 2:35 (November 12, 1746).
46. Wesley, *Works* (Jackson) 2:208 (September 19, 1750).
47. Wesley, *Works* (Jackson) 4:226 (April 26, 1782).

human help, I knew of no remedy but prayer. Immediately the lameness was gone, and he went just as he did before."[48] Another time, he "set out for Derby; but the smith had so effectually lamed one of my horses, that many told me he would never be able to travel more. I thought, 'Even this may be made matter of prayer;' and set out cheerfully. The horse, instead of growing worse and worse, went better and better; and in the afternoon (after I had preached at Leek by the way) brought me safe to Derby."[49]

Prayer was also effective in the healing of more extreme illnesses. "I visited Mr. Maxfield, struck with a violent stroke of palsy. He was senseless, and seemed near death; but we besought God for him, and his spirit revived, I cannot but think, in answer to prayer."[50] In a letter to one of his correspondents (responding to a letter that no longer survives), Wesley writes, "It really seems had it not been for the mighty power of prayer the boy would have been blind all his life."[51] Here it appears that God even healed blindness, either through Wesley's prayers, or the prayers of other believers Wesley knew.

The ultimate enemy was death. Although Wesley never claimed to have raised anyone from the dead, he testified to the power of prayer to deliver those who were on the very brink of death. In his journal, Wesley mentions "a gentleman who had little thought of God, till his favourite child lay at the point of death. It then came into his mind, to pray for his life. He did so, and the child recovered. This struck him to the heart, and he rested no more, till his own soul was healed."[52] Wesley's own prayers had aided in the recovery of some of these: "When I came home, they told me the Physician said, he did not expect Mr. Meyrick would live till the morning. I went to him, but his pulse was gone. He had been speechless and senseless for some time. A few of us immediately joined in prayer: (I relate the naked fact:) Before we had done, his sense and his speech returned. Now, he that will account for this by natural causes has my free leave: But I choose to say, This is the power of God."[53] In another instance, he went to call at the house of a poor man: "I found him and his wife sick in one bed, and with small hopes of the recovery of either. Yet (after prayer) I believed they would 'not die, but live,

48. Wesley, *Works* (Jackson) 4:216 (September 5, 1781).
49. Wesley, *Works* (Jackson) 4:247 (May 23, 1783).
50. Wesley, *Works* (Jackson) 4:242 (December 21, 1782).
51. Wesley to Peter Garforth, August 9, 1783, 187.
52. Wesley, *Works* (Jackson) 2:437 (March 23, 1758).
53. Wesley, *Works* (Jackson) 1:406 (December 20, 1742).

and declare the loving-kindness of the Lord.' The next time I called, he was sitting below stairs, and his wife able to go abroad."[54]

Lest these accounts sound too triumphalistic, one must balance them against the faith-filled declarations he made in the late 1780s when his brother Charles Wesley was sick: "I do not depend upon physicians, but upon Him that raiseth the dead. Only let your whole family stir themselves up and be instant in Prayer; then I have only to say to each, 'If thou canst believe, thou shalt see the glory of God!'"[55] Not three days later, he wrote, "But above all let prayer be made continually; and probably he will be stronger after this illness than he has been these ten years."[56] Only nine days after he wrote these words, Charles Wesley died. The failure of these prayers and exhortations in no wise dims the remarkable answers to prayer Wesley did receive during his life. Both his faith and his practice highlight his belief in the miraculous intervening power of God in human life.

Demonic Affliction

Despite the testimony of Wesley's sermon "A Caution Against Bigotry" wherein he comments, "No man now *casts out devils*,"[57] his journals clearly depict those with demonic afflictions being brought to peace through prayer. In 1739, he was asked to visit a young woman of "nineteen or twenty years." Wesley described the scene in borderline-lurid detail: "I found her on the bed, two or three persons holding her. It was a terrible sight. Anguish, horror, and despair, above all description, appeared in her pale face. The thousand distortions of her whole body showed how the dogs of hell were gnawing her heart. The shrieks intermixed were scarce to be endured." She screamed out, "I am the devil's now" and "began praying [to] the devil."[58] Whenever she lapsed into silence, "another young woman began to roar out as loud as she had done."[59] John and Charles Wesley prayed with them for two hours, with the result that "God in a moment spoke peace into the soul,

---

54. Wesley, *Works* (Jackson) 1:482 (January 14, 1745).
55. Wesley to Charles Wesley, March 17, 1788, 46.
56. Wesley to Sarah Wesley, March 20, 1788, 49.
57. Wesley, "Sermon 38," 479.
58. Wesley, *Works* (Jackson) 1:234–35 (October 23, 1739).
59. Wesley, *Works* (Jackson) 1:235 (October 23, 1739).

first of the first tormented, and then of the other. And they both joined in singing praise to Him who had 'stilled the enemy and the avenger.'"[60]

This proved to be a short-lived reprieve, however. Four days later, the summons came again, for the first young woman was again in the grip of demonic forces. When Wesley arrived, "She burst out into a horrid laughter, and said, 'No power, no power; no faith, no faith. She is mine; her soul is mine. I have her, and will not let her go.'"[61] Wesley and the others there prayed and "begged of God to increase our faith," until the woman was freed enough to sing the doxology.[62] The next day Wesley visited the two women again, and found them once more under demonic power. "The violent convulsions all over their bodies were such as words cannot describe. Their cries and groans were too horrid to be borne."[63] Wesley and the others there prayed through the evening until one o'clock in the morning, when the first woman was able to cry out to the Lord Jesus for help, which she continued to do for "the greatest part of the night."[64]

That same week, Wesley went to another one who had "taken ill." When he arrived, the woman "lay on the ground, furiously gnashing her teeth, and after a while roared aloud. It was not easy for three or four persons to hold her, especially when the name of Jesus was named. We prayed; the violence of her symptoms ceased, though without a complete deliverance."[65] Wesley went home but was sent for again later that evening. He describes this second encounter: "She began screaming before I came into the room; then broke out into a horrid laughter, mixed with blasphemy, grievous to hear."[66] John and Charles Wesley stayed with her for two hours with little progress. They returned the next day, and "now it was that God showed He heareth the prayer. All her pangs ceased in a moment: She was filled with peace, and knew that the son of wickedness was departed from her."[67]

A little over a year later, in 1741, Wesley "met with a surprising instance of the power of the devil."[68] A woman, sitting at home, had

60. Wesley, *Works* (Jackson) 1:235 (October 23, 1739).
61. Wesley, *Works* (Jackson) 1:236–37 (October 27, 1739).
62. Wesley, *Works* (Jackson) 1:237 (October 27, 1739).
63. Wesley, *Works* (Jackson) 1:237 (October 28, 1739).
64. Wesley, *Works* (Jackson) 1:237 (October 28, 1739).
65. Wesley, *Works* (Jackson) 1:236 (October 25, 1739).
66. Wesley, *Works* (Jackson) 1:236 (October 25, 1739).
67. Wesley, *Works* (Jackson) 1:236 (October 26, 1739).
68. Wesley, *Works* (Jackson) 1:295 (January 11, 1741).

suddenly thrown the Bible away, saying that she was "good enough" and needed neither the Bible nor prayer anymore. Wesley came to speak with her, and she said, "I am saved; I ail nothing; I am happy."[69] Wesley, however, was unconvinced. He writes, "Yet it was easy to discern, she was in the most violent agony, both of body and mind; sweating exceedingly, notwithstanding the severe frost, and not continuing in the same posture a moment."[70] When Wesley and his companions began to pray, "she raged beyond measure; but soon sunk down as dead. In a few minutes she revived, and joined in prayer."[71] The next day, however, she was "in a violent agony" again. Many came to see her, but "to every one of whom she spoke, concerning either their actual or their heart sins, and that so closely that several of them went away in more haste than they came."[72] Wesley was sent for again, but before he arrived, she was able to testify, "The peace of God is come to my soul. I know that my Redeemer liveth."[73] For several days thereafter, "her mouth was filled with [Christ's] praise, and her 'talk was wholly of his wondrous works.'"[74]

Sometimes, what Wesley understood as a demonic affliction was understood by others as mental illness. In 1755, a young attorney "fell raving mad.... He sung, and swore, and screamed, and cursed, and blasphemed, as if possessed by legion."[75] When Wesley arrived, he began to calm down. "I sat down on the bed, and he was still. Soon after he fell into tears and prayer. We prayed with him and left him calm for the present."[76] In another instance, Wesley writes, "I went to a young woman who was some days since suddenly struck with what they call madness; and so it was, but a diabolical madness, as plainly appeared from numerous circumstances: However, after we had been at prayer, she fell asleep, and never raged or blasphemed after."[77]

Finally, on one occasion at a house, "a young woman came in (who had received remission of sins) all in tears, and in deep anguish of spirit.

---

69. Wesley, *Works* (Jackson) 1:296 (January 12, 1741).
70. Wesley, *Works* (Jackson) 1:296 (January 12, 1741).
71. Wesley, *Works* (Jackson) 1:296 (January 12, 1741).
72. Wesley, *Works* (Jackson) 1:296 (January 13, 1741).
73. Wesley, *Works* (Jackson) 1:296 (January 13, 1741).
74. Wesley, *Works* (Jackson) 1:296 (January 13, 1741).
75. Wesley, *Works* (Jackson) 2:343 (September 7, 1755).
76. Wesley, *Works* (Jackson) 2:343 (September 7, 1755).
77. Wesley, *Works* (Jackson) 2:491 (July 1, 1759).

She said she had been in torment all night by reasoning, and verily believed the devil had possession of her again. In the midst of our prayers she cried out, 'He is gone, he is gone: I again rejoice in God my Saviour.'"[78] Wesley relied on prayer, faith, and the redeeming power of God to deliver people from demonic affliction. Often, this deliverance did not come quickly, but only after hours, or even days, of prayer. Wesley was persistent, however, and often saw the deliverance he sought.

Conclusion

Wesley expected to encounter the supernatural in his life. He believed his family's accounts of a poltergeist that haunted their rectory, although he had his own explanation for why it was there. His theology expected God to work miracles and heal people when he prayed, and he claimed several instances of both divine healings and other miracles in his life. He also understood the gift of tongues to have ceased, but attributed that to the faithlessness of Christians rather than the timing of God. Finally, he encountered a number of people who evidenced demonic affliction and struggled persistently in prayer until he saw them freed. Wesley's practice demonstrated a thoroughgoing supernatural worldview, which encompassed his theology of prayer.

---

78. Wesley to James Hutton, May 7, 1739, 305.

— 10 —

Prayer and Revival

John Wesley considered revival a supernatural manifestation of God's grace. This chapter examines the role prayer played in the revival that flourished under Wesley's preaching. First, prayer was the central element in both the initiation and preservation of revival. Next, prayer was the central action taken, both by the ones touched by conviction and desiring assurance, and by those ministering to them. Sometimes this resulted in strong groans, cries, and trembling; other times in dreams, visions, or other sense impressions. Finally, this chapter examines Wesley's attempt to find a balance, bringing correction to the extremes of enthusiasm while refusing to quench the Spirit in legitimate (but disruptive) expressions of God's conviction and power.

Initiating Revival

Revival, in Wesley's understanding, was a divinely given awakening of human hearts toward God. As such, revival could not properly be understood as "initiated" by humans, but humans could use the means of grace to wait upon God's divine timing. Of these, the chief means was prayer. Wesley writes, "Supposing we could pray in faith for the accomplishment of the promise which is given in the last chapter of St. Mark, there is no doubt it would be fulfilled now as it was seventeen hundred years ago. And I have known many instances of this both in England and elsewhere."[1]

These "many instances" convinced Wesley that God's desire was to bring revival everywhere that needed it. He encourages his correspondents to await revival faithfully in prayer, whatever their location: "If you continue instant in prayer, I trust there will be such a work in Cornwall as never was yet."[2] He also writes, "By meekness, gentleness, and patience, with faith and prayer, you will prevail at Torrington also."[3] This was not confined to England or the British Isles, either. He wrote to William Black (then ministering in Halifax), described the continually increasing work of God in England, and encouraged him in his own work: "The same thing I am in hopes you will now see in America likewise. See that you expect it, and that you seek for it in His appointed ways—namely, with fasting and unintermitted prayer. And take care that you be not at all discouraged, though you should not always have an immediate answer. You know 'His manner and times are best.' Therefore pray always! Pray, and faint not."[4]

Although prayer in general was important, the place where Wesley laid the most emphasis was prayer meetings. He observed that, whatever other activity did or did not happen, the presence of consistent prayer meetings often led to revival, saying, "In every place there is a remarkable blessing attending the meetings for prayer. A revival of the work of God is generally the consequence of them. The most prevailing fault among the Methodists is to be *too outward* in religion. We are continually forgetting that the kingdom of God is *within us*, and that our fundamental principle is, We are saved *by faith*, producing all *inward* holiness, not by works, by any externals whatever."[5] This connection could clearly be seen by tracing the progress of revival from those who were spiritually awakened in a prayer meeting to the rest of the congregation: "I suppose the prayer-meetings still continue? In many places they have been of more use than even the preaching. And in them the flame first broke out which afterwards spread through the whole people. You have, I hope, more than one or two at those meetings who use the gift which God has given them. And if they pray for the *whole gospel*

---

1. Wesley to James Currie, February 19, 1788, 37.
2. Wesley to Joseph Taylor, September 9, 1782, 138.
3. Wesley to Samuel Bardsley, March 27, 1790, 209.
4. Wesley to William Black, November 26, 1786, 352.
5. Wesley to John Valton, November 12, 1771, 289.

salvation, God will send a gracious answer down."[6] Nor did prayer meetings have to be big. The important factor to successful prayer meetings was faith and commitment: "If two or three of you continue instant in prayer, the work will revive at Trowbridge also. When you are met together, boldly lay hold on the promise: His word will speak, and will not lie."[7]

Preserving Revival

The presence of revival did not signal the successful conclusion of the prayer meetings; on the contrary, Wesley advises their faithful continuance as a means of preserving the revival fire: "I am glad to hear that your Society prospers and that the work of God continues to increase in the town. It always will if prayer-meetings are kept up (without interfering with the classes and bands)."[8] Two years later, he gives the same advice to someone else: "But the grand means of the revival of the work of God in Sheffield was the prayer-meetings. There were then twelve of them in various parts of the town every Sunday night. Keep up these, and you will keep up the flame."[9]

Even with prayer meetings, though, the pattern Wesley observed was that revival tended, over time, to die down. In light of that, Wesley also extolled the importance of private prayer. "I do not wonder at all that, after that great and extraordinary work of God, there should be a remarkable decay. So we have found it in almost all places. A swift increase is generally followed by a decrease equally swift. All we can do to prevent it is continually to exhort all who have tasted that the Lord is gracious to remember our Lord's words, 'Watch and pray that ye enter not into temptation.'"[10] Unfortunately, sometimes believers entered into temptation, and the revival fire was lost. On one occasion when Wesley visited Kingswood School, he recollects, "I found there had been a fresh revival of the work of God among them some months ago: But it was soon at an end, which I impute chiefly to their total neglect of private prayer. Without this, all the other means which they enjoyed could profit them nothing."[11] In addition, obstacles to revival came from outside the church as well.

6. Wesley to Ann Bolton, January 5, 1783, 162.
7. Wesley to Mary Cooke, December 21, 1787, 28.
8. Wesley to Hannah Ball, April 13, 1786, 324.
9. Wesley to Edward Jackson, October 24, 1788, 99.
10. Wesley to William Black, July 13, 1783, 182.
11. Wesley, *Works* (Jackson) 3:479 (September 4, 1772).

Hecklers were a frequent barrier to new revival. Agitators, looking for easy entertainment or upset at the religious ideas the Methodists were presenting, would interrupt the services with shouts, catcalls, and other disruptions. Wesley found prayer to be a means of combatting them. When hecklers interrupted one service, he notes, "We all began singing a psalm, which put them utterly to silence. We then poured out our souls in prayer for them, and they appeared altogether confounded."[12] In another instance, a woman began heckling Wesley during a service: "The instant she broke out, I turned full upon her, and declared the love our Lord had for *her* soul. We then prayed that He would confirm the word of his grace. She was struck to the heart; and shame covered her face."[13]

Far more disruptive and dangerous than hecklers were the mobs. Wesley and his preachers frequently found themselves at the mercy of mobs of angry villagers, violently opposed to the presence of these Methodists in their town. Several times, Wesley found refuge in prayer when facing a mob. He writes, "As I was meeting the Leaders, a company of young men, having prepared themselves by strong drink, broke open the door, and came rushing in with the utmost fury. I began praying for them immediately; not one opened his mouth, or lifted up a finger against us: And after half an hour, we all went away together, in great quietness and love."[14] This happened more than once. "I was writing at Francis Ward's, in the afternoon, when the cry arose, that the mob had beset the house. We prayed that God would disperse them; and it was so: One went this way, and another that; so that, in half an hour, not a man was left."[15]

Once, when Wesley visited a shut-in gentlewoman, "the house was beset on all sides by an innumerable multitude of people."[16] The residents of the house tried in vain to calm the crowd, who cried out loudly for the Methodists to be brought out to them. They soon "forced open the outer door, and filled the passage. Only a wainscot-partition was between us, which was not likely to stand long." One young lady "cried out, 'O Sir, what must we do?' I said, 'We must pray.'"[17] When they broke through, Wesley immediately confronted them, and talked down the leaders, until he

12. Wesley, *Works* (Jackson) 1:199 (June 7, 1739).
13. Wesley, *Works* (Jackson) 1:283 (August 4, 1740).
14. Wesley, *Works* (Jackson) 1:417 (March 18, 1743).
15. Wesley, *Works* (Jackson) 1:436 (October 20, 1743).
16. Wesley, *Works* (Jackson) 1:504 (July 4, 1745).
17. Wesley, *Works* (Jackson) 1:504 (July 4, 1745).

was able to leave safely. He reflected, "Who can deny that God heareth the prayer, or that he hath all power in heaven and earth?"[18]

Another time, a drunk mob chased him from the preaching-house to the home in which he was staying, "throwing dirt, stones, and clods in abundance."[19] One of the leaders of the mob followed Wesley and his friends into the house, and discovered to his surprise that none of the rest of the mob followed him in, so he was shut in with Wesley as the mob continued to throw stones through the windows. "A large stone struck him on the forehead, and the blood spouted out like a stream. He cried out, 'O Sir, are we to die to-night? What must I do? What must I do?' I said, 'Pray to God. He is able to deliver you from all danger.' He took my advice, and began praying in such a manner as he had scarce done ever since he was born."[20] Wesley and his companion then "went to prayer," and as the mob broke through the front door, the two of them walked unnoticed out the back door.

Conviction and Assurance

Two central elements of Wesley's revival were conviction of sin and assurance of salvation. Sinners, he believed, would be convicted of their sins, whether through the preaching or directly by the power of the Holy Spirit, and would feel an agony that expressed itself emotionally, physically, or both. This was followed by prayer, certainly by the one convicted, and often by Wesley or others nearby. After some time—sometimes minutes, sometimes hours or even days—the one convicted would feel a supernatural assurance of salvation, and the agony of conviction would turn into the joy of praise.

The following example demonstrates the main features of this pattern, but also shows that the process was frequently an interruption to the planned work: "In the afternoon, one who had tasted the love of God, but had turned again to folly, was deeply convinced, and torn, as it were, in pieces, by guilt, and remorse, and fear; and even after the sermon was ended, she continued in the same agony, it seemed, both of body and soul. Many of us were then met together in another part of the house; but her cries were so piercing, though at a distance, that I could not pray, nor

---

18. Wesley, *Works* (Jackson) 1:505 (July 4, 1745).
19. Wesley, *Works* (Jackson) 2:83 (February 12, 1748).
20. Wesley, *Works* (Jackson) 2:83 (February 12, 1748).

hardly speak, being quite chilled every time I heard them."[21] Those who had gathered together discussed what they ought to do and decided at length to bring her in and pray for her. "She was brought in, and we cried to God, to heal her backsliding. We soon found we were asking according to his will. He not only had her 'depart in peace,' but filled many others, till then heavy of heart, with peace and joy in believing."[22] Despite the peace and joy that marked the ending, the process as a whole was clearly disturbing to Wesley, at least in this instance.

Often, this would happen, not just to individuals, but to entire groups. "As soon as I began to speak, some of them burst into tears, and their emotion rose higher and higher; but it was kept within bounds till I began to pray. A cry then arose, which spread from one to another, till almost all cried aloud for mercy, and would not be comforted."[23] When so many were struck with conviction, Wesley sought out the ones who, he deemed, needed help the most, and prayed for them. "After speaking a few words, I went to prayer. A cry began, and soon spread through the whole company; so that my voice was lost. Two seemed to be distressed above all the rest. We continued wrestling with God, till one of them had a good hope, and the other was 'filled with joy and peace in believing.'"[24] Even in less public, more intimate circumstances, God ministered to people gathered together. "[A man] and his wife were present, where a few were met for prayer. Her sorrow was soon turned into joy. Her husband, who was before little awakened, was just then cut to the heart, and felt the wrath of God abiding on him: Nor did he cease crying to God, till his prayers and tears were swallowed up in thanksgiving."[25]

The timing of deliverance from conviction and receiving the comfort of assurance was unpredictable and appeared to vary widely from person to person. "While I was speaking a woman dropped down before me, and presently a second and third, and one after another five others. . . . Upon praying, five of them were comforted, one continued in pain an hour longer, and one for two or three days."[26] On other occasions, even intense prayer did not deliver them: "At eight two persons were in strong pain; but though

21. Wesley, *Works* (Jackson) 1:365 (April 18, 1742).
22. Wesley, *Works* (Jackson) 1:365 (April 18, 1742).
23. Wesley, *Works* (Jackson) 3:452 (January 17, 1772).
24. Wesley, *Works* (Jackson) 3:78 (January 6, 1762).
25. Wesley, *Works* (Jackson) 3:107 (July 29, 1762).
26. Wesley to James Hutton, July 2, 1739, 325.

we cried to God, there was no answer, neither did He deliver them at all."[27] Wesley makes no attempt to explain or theorize about these situations; he merely notes them and moves on, leaving the process of God's workings in the human heart shrouded in divine mystery.

Revival Manifestations

The overall structure of conviction, prayer, and assurance forms a convincing pattern to describe the events in Wesley's revival, but sometimes other elements would surface within this pattern. Sometimes the agony of conviction would be accompanied by groaning, trembling, falling, or similar disruptions. When these initially came, alongside the conviction of sin, they caught Wesley off guard. In the course of two weeks of ministry in 1739, he experienced a number of these incidents. On Tuesday, April 17, Wesley preached and called upon God to confirm his word: "Immediately one that stood by (to our no small surprise) cried out aloud, with the utmost vehemence, even as in the agonies of death. But we continued in prayer, till 'a new song was put in her mouth, a thanksgiving unto our God.' Soon after, two other persons (well known in this place, as labouring to live in all good conscience towards all men) were seized with strong pain, and constrained to 'roar for the disquietness of their heart.' But it was not long before they likewise burst forth into praise to God their Savior."[28]

That Saturday, "a young man was suddenly seized with a violent trembling all over, and in a few minutes, the sorrows of his heart being enlarged, sunk down to the ground. But we ceased not calling upon God, till he raised him up full of 'peace and joy in the Holy Ghost.'"[29] The following Thursday, Wesley felt prompted, with no prior plan, "to declare strongly and explicitly, that God 'willeth all men to be' thus 'saved;' and to pray, that, 'if this were not the truth of God, he would not suffer the blind to go out of the way; but, if it were, he would bear witness to his word.' Immediately one, and another, and another sunk to the earth: They dropped on every side as thunderstruck. One of them cried aloud."[30]

As these events recurred in his services, onlookers became critical. The next Tuesday, two weeks after the first incident, as Wesley recalls, "A

27. Wesley to James Hutton, August 15, 1739, 332.
28. Wesley, *Works* (Jackson) 1:187 (April 17, 1739).
29. Wesley, *Works* (Jackson) 1:187–88 (April 21, 1739).
30. Wesley, *Works* (Jackson) 1:188 (April 26, 1739).

Quaker, who stood by, was not a little displeased at the dissimulation [i.e., fakery] of those creatures, and was biting his lips and knitting his brows, when he dropped down as thunderstruck. The agony he was in was even terrible to behold. We besought God not to lay folly to his charge. And he soon lifted up his head and cried aloud, 'Now I know, thou art a prophet of the Lord.'"[31]

Wesley was well aware that these demonstrations of the flesh, or manifestations of the Spirit, were offending onlookers. "Some sunk down, and there remained no strength in them; others exceedingly trembled and quaked: Some were torn with a kind of convulsive motion in every part of their bodies, and that so violently, that often four or five persons could not hold one of them. I have seen many hysterical and many epileptic fits; but none of them were like these, in many respects. I immediately prayed, that God would not suffer those who were weak to be offended."[32] Wesley certainly considered the possibility that these incidents were equally a demonstration of human foolishness, and appears to have initially leaned in that direction, if only temporarily.

In fact, the day after he prayed that the weak would not be offended, he met with his society at Fetter Lane where they together confessed that they had sinned "above all, by blaspheming his work among us, imputing it either to nature, to the force of imagination and animal spirits, or even to the delusion of the devil."[33] In this, Wesley returned to the position he had recorded in his journal a month prior. In that entry, he had argued that judgment of such manifestations should not be made "in the moment," but only after a season, and that based on the measure of life-change wrought in the individual:

> What I have to say touching visions or dreams, is this: I know several persons in whom this great change was wrought in a dream, or during a strong representation to the eye of their mind, of Christ either on the cross, or in glory. This is the fact; let any judge of it as they please. And that such a change was then wrought, appears (not from their shedding tears only, or falling into fits, or crying out: These are not the fruits, as you seem to suppose, whereby I

---

31. Wesley, *Works* (Jackson) 1:190 (May 1, 1739).
32. Wesley, *Works* (Jackson) 1:204 (June 15, 1739).
33. Wesley, *Works* (Jackson) 1:204 (June 16, 1739).

judge, but) from the whole tenor of their life, till then, many ways wicked; from that time, holy, just, and good.[34]

By the end of that year (1739), Wesley answered to Bishop Butler for these irregularities in his services, writing, "BB: I hear, too, many people fall into fits in your societies, and that you pray over them. JW: I do so, my lord. When any show by strong cries and tears that their soul is in deep anguish, I frequently pray to God to deliver them from it. And our prayer is often answered in that hour."[35]

As the revival continued, however, the manifestations continued. In certain cases, Wesley judged they warranted a rebuke. The first of these are cases in which the very foundations of Christian doctrine were threatened. In 1741, Wesley wrote, "A spirit of enthusiasm was breaking in upon many, who charged their own imaginations on the will of God, and that not written, but impressed on their hearts. If these impressions be received as the rule of action, instead of the written word, I know nothing so wicked or absurd but we may fall into, and that without remedy."[36]

The second situation where Wesley judged manifestations warranted rebuke was when they became so extravagant and extreme as to pass into sheer nonsense. Wesley had a very low tolerance for what he called "enthusiasm," and when the manifestations appeared to pass into mere fanaticism, he did not hesitate to rebuke them. In September of 1742, he wrote of some claims of supernatural experience:

> I approved of their experience, (because agreeable to the written Word,) as to their feeling the working of the Spirit of God, in peace, and joy, and love. But as to what some of them said farther, concerning feeling the blood of Christ running upon their arms, or going down their throat, or poured like warm water upon their breast or heart; I plainly told them, the utmost I could allow, without renouncing both Scripture and reason, was, that some of these circumstances might be from God (though I could not affirm they were) working in an unusual manner, no way essential either to justification or sanctification; but that all the rest I must believe to be the mere empty dreams of an heated imagination.[37]

---

34. Wesley, *Works* (Jackson) 1:195 (May 20, 1739).

35. Wesley, *Works* (Bicentennial) 19:472.

36. Wesley, *Works* (Jackson) 1:318 (July 13, 1741). See also "Guidance," in chapter 8 of this book.

37. Wesley, *Works* (Jackson) 1:397 (September 6, 1742).

Sometimes this nonsense became so ridiculous as to cross into comedy. In December of 1742, Wesley writes, a man "who had received a sense of the love of God a few days before, came riding through the town, hallooing and shouting, and driving all the people before him; telling them, God had told him he should be a king, and should tread all his enemies under his feet. I sent him home immediately to his work, and advised him to cry day and night to God, that he might be lowly in heart; lest Satan should again get an advantage over him."[38] Despite the apparent humor, Wesley immediately discerned the serious danger to this man's soul in the foolishness, and straightaway directed him to its remedy: honest work and continuous night-and-day prayer.

A few years later, in 1744, a pamphlet appeared titled *Observations upon the Conduct and Behaviour of a Certain Sect usually distinguished by the Name of Methodists*. In this pamphlet, the anonymous author puts a question to Wesley: "Whether a due and regular attendance on the public offices of religion, paid by good men in a serious and composed way, does not better answer the true ends of devotion, and is not a better evidence of the co-operation of the Holy Spirit, than those sudden agonies, roarings, screamings, tremblings, droppings down, ravings, and madnesses, into which their hearers have been cast."[39] In his reply, Wesley continued to defend the revival, along with the (less extreme) manifestations. He answers,

> (1). There is no manner of need to set the one in opposition to the other; seeing we continually exhort all who attend on our preaching to attend the offices of the Church. And they do pay a more regular attendance there than ever they did before. (2). Their attending the Church did not, in fact, answer those ends at all till they attended this preaching also. (3). It is the preaching of remission of sins through Jesus Christ, which alone answers the true ends of devotion. And this will always be accompanied with the co-operation of the Holy Spirit; though not always with sudden agonies, roarings, screamings, tremblings, or droppings down. Indeed, if God is pleased at any time to permit any of these, I cannot hinder it. Neither can this hinder the work of his Spirit in the soul; which may be carried on either with or without them. But, (4). I cannot apprehend it to be any reasonable proof that "this is not the work of God" that a convinced sinner should "fall into an extreme agony, both of body and soul;" that another

---

38. Wesley, *Works* (Jackson) 1:404 (December 4, 1742).
39. Wesley, *Farther Appeal, Part I*, 61.

should "roar for the disquietness of her heart;" that others should scream or "cry with a loud and bitter cry, 'What must we do to be saved?'"; that others should "exceedingly tremble and quake"; and others, in a deep sense of the majesty of God, "should fall prostrate upon the ground."[40]

Fifteen years later, in 1759, Wesley reflected back on the early days of the revival, and how attitudes had changed since then, especially regarding the "extraordinary circumstances" of manifestations, in which he acknowledges the whole panoply of possible origins for them:

> The danger *was*, to regard extraordinary circumstances too much, such as outcries, convulsions, visions, trances; as if these were essential to the inward work, so that it could not go on without them. Perhaps the danger *is*, to regard them too little, to condemn them altogether; to imagine they had nothing of God in them, and were an hindrance to his work. Whereas the truth is, 1. God suddenly and strongly convinced many that they were lost sinners; the natural consequence whereof were sudden outcries and strong bodily convulsions: 2. To strengthen and encourage them that believed, and to make his work more apparent, he favored several of them with divine dreams, others with trances and visions: 3. In some of these instances, after a time, nature mixed with grace: 4. Satan likewise mimicked this work of God, in order to discredit the whole work: And yet it is not wise to give up this part, any more than to give up the whole. At first it was, doubtless, wholly from God. It is partly so at this day; and he will enable us to discern how far, in every case, the work is pure, and where it mixes or degenerates.
>
> Let us even suppose that in some few cases there was a mixture of dissimulation; that persons pretended to see or feel what they did not, and imitated the cries or convulsive motions of those who were really overpowered by the Spirit of God: Yet even this should not make us either deny or undervalue the real work of the Spirit. The shadow is no disparagement of the substance, nor the counterfeit of the real diamond.
>
> We may farther suppose, that Satan will make these visions an occasion of pride: But what can be inferred from hence? Nothing, but that we should guard against it; that we should diligently exhort all to be little in their own eyes, knowing that nothing avails

---

40. Wesley, *Farther Appeal*, Part I, 62.

with God but humble love. But still, to slight or censure visions in general, would be both irrational and unchristian.[41]

Conclusion

Wesley firmly believed in the power of prayer, especially in organized prayer meetings, to initiate revival in an area, as he took for granted God's willingness to bring revival as a scriptural promise. Likewise, prayer and prayer meetings were indispensable to him for preserving revivals, both against internal obstacles of temptation and complacency, and external obstacles of hecklers and mobs. Those who experienced the conviction of God in his revivals and desired the assurance of salvation were to seek it through prayer. Likewise, those who ministered to them were to minister through prayer. In the process, people sometimes exhibited the work of the Spirt through groans, cries, trembling, and other supernatural manifestations. Wesley labored to keep from quenching the Spirit, but when these extraordinary circumstances began to be taken to dangerous extremes, Wesley called them back to the word of God and prayer.

---

41. Wesley, *Works* (Jackson) 2:519–20 (November 25, 1759).

— 11 —

Prayer and Mystic Quietism

THIS CHAPTER EXAMINES HOW Wesley's conception of mysticism changed over time. Early in his life, he became enamored with mystic Quietism and the mystic's search for union with God. Over time, as the flaws of mystic Quietism became clearer to Wesley, he eventually abandoned it. Before long, he actively began opposing Quietism as a distraction from true, biblical Christianity. The means of grace, especially prayer, were an important element in his understanding of biblical Christianity, and he was impressed with the Moravian commitment to continual prayer that he witnessed on a trip to Germany. Unfortunately, the Moravian teachings began to embrace Quietism, and despite great reluctance, Wesley began to separate from the Moravians over this difference.

Experiments in Mystic Quietism

Wesley had been introduced to mysticism early on, as his mother Susanna was well acquainted with several mystic writers.[1] In 1725, while he was at Christ Church College, Oxford, he was "introduced to Jeremy Taylor's *Rules for Holy Living* and Thomas à Kempis's *Imitation of Christ*."[2] For the next decade, Wesley embarked on a number of what Robert Tuttle calls "mystical

1. Tuttle, *Mysticism*, 48–49.
2. Tuttle, *Mysticism*, 55.

experiments."³ At Oxford, Wesley undertook to live fully a life of holiness and commitment to God.⁴ A couple of years later, when Wesley moved to Wroot as a curate and then as a priest, he sought solitude and immersed himself in mystic writings and the practice of "ejaculatory prayers," short prayers said often (at least hourly) in lieu of a dedicated prayer time.⁵ When he was called back to Oxford in 1729, he joined the Holy Club his brother Charles had started. There, in addition to charitable works, he focused on an ascetic lifestyle and pursued the interior life of mystical contemplation.⁶ Finally, in 1735, he headed to Georgia, anticipating a wilderness that would aid his mystic disciplines. Instead, he found himself busy managing a congregation in the settlement of Frederica.⁷ He was frustrated and discouraged with his apparent lack of progress in spiritual discipline; he felt he had "no faith, no peace, and no assurance."⁸

Tuttle identified a major shift in Wesley's attitude toward mysticism that took place in three stages. The first stage, in 1736, began with the question of the means of grace in the Christian life. The second stage, in 1738, was a reexamination of the issue and a questioning of the idea of the dark night of the soul. The last stage, later in 1738, was the question of the atonement in mystic theology. This stage culminated in his experience at Aldersgate.

Questioning Mystic Quietism

John Wesley's change of heart concerning mysticism began with the issue of the means of grace. In 1736, he wrote a letter to his brother Samuel Wesley claiming that "the rock on which I had the nearest made shipwreck of my faith was the writings of the Mystics; under which term I comprehend all, and only those, who slight any of the means of grace."⁹ In the letter, John Wesley includes a "short scheme of their doctrines," which served to encapsulate the points he was finding objectionable. The overall theme of these objectionable points was the devaluing of the means of grace.

3. Tuttle, *Mysticism*, 65.
4. Tuttle, *Mysticism*, 67.
5. Tuttle, *Mysticism*, 73.
6. Tuttle, *Mysticism*, 76–77.
7. Tuttle, *Mysticism*, 87.
8. Tuttle, *Mysticism*, 90.
9. Wesley to Samuel Wesley Jr., November 23, 1736, 207.

According to John Wesley's scheme, mystics teach that "love is attained by them who are . . . entered into the passive state."[10] Having attained the end, they "use all outward means only as they are moved thereto," and this only for secondary reasons, and "not as necessary or helpful to them."[11] Perhaps most importantly, "Public prayer, or any forms, they need not; for they pray without ceasing. Sensible devotion in any prayer they despise, it being a great hindrance to perfection."[12]

Likewise, mystics cease to read Scripture, take the Lord's Supper, or fast. This passivity applied equally to those providing spiritual direction for seekers; the seekers were not to be advised or encouraged to engage in any spiritual disciplines. In fact, the scheme was laissez-faire about the eternal souls of the unbelieving, as well: "If one who was religious falls off, let him alone. Either a man is converted to God, or not: if he is not, his own will must guide him, in spite of all you can do; if he is, he is so guided by the Spirit of God as not to need your direction."[13] Not only the means of grace, but works of godliness were disparaged. "As to doing good, take care of yourself first. . . . Beware of . . . an eager desire to set others a good example. . . . Beware of a zeal to do great things for God. . . . The command of doing good concerns not you yet."[14]

However, this was just the beginning of Wesley's change of heart toward mysticism. The shift was incremental; he was soon reading the mystics again. Early in 1738, he read the works of St. Cyprian, who convinced him that what the mystics termed the "dark night of the soul" was not a necessary stage of spiritual growth to be received passively, but a manifestation of one's own "fear and doubt" that was to be fought.[15] Much later in life, he still fought against this idea: "Your state of mind for some time has been that which the Papists very improperly term a state of Desertion; wherein they suppose God *deserts* or forsakes the soul only for *His* own will and pleasure! But this is absolutely impossible: I deny that such a state ever existed under the sun."[16] He ascribed this state of mind to other causes entirely: "The trouble you feel is . . . a natural effect of disordered liver, of the corruptible

---

10. Wesley to Samuel Wesley Jr., November 23, 1736, 208.
11. Wesley to Samuel Wesley Jr., November 23, 1736, 208.
12. Wesley to Samuel Wesley Jr., November 23, 1736, 208.
13. Wesley to Samuel Wesley Jr., November 23, 1736, 209.
14. Wesley to Samuel Wesley Jr., November 23, 1736, 210.
15. Tuttle, *Mysticism*, 98.
16. Wesley to Ann Bolton, April 24, 1777, 261.

body pressing down the soul. But you must likewise take into the account preternatural influence. For you may be assured your grand adversary will not be forgetful to avail himself of the opportunity, sometimes by plausible suggestions, sometimes by horrid and grievous injections."[17]

Furthermore, Wesley began to complain once again about the mystic denial of the means of grace.[18] In a personal memorandum he wrote to chronicle his spiritual condition, he considered the influence of the mystics in his life: "I grew acquainted with the mystic writers, whose noble descriptions of union with God and internal religion made everything else appear mean, flat, and insipid. . . . But alas! It was nothing like that religion which Christ and his apostles lived and taught."[19] The central problem, once again, was a denial of the means of grace. "The form ran thus: 'Love is all; all the commands beside are only means of love; you must choose those which you feel are means to you and use them as long as they are so.' Thus were all the bands burst at once."[20] Although the result in Wesley's life was not to cast away all means of grace, "yet, I know not how, I fluctuated between obedience and disobedience: I had no heart, no vigour, no zeal in obeying; continually doubting whether I was right or wrong, and never out of perplexities and entanglements."[21] Wesley concludes, "All the other enemies of Christianity are triflers; the mystics are the most dangerous of all its enemies. They stab it in the vitals, and its most serious professors are most likely to fall by them. May I praise him who hath snatched me out of this fire likewise, by warning all others that it is set on fire of hell."[22]

The final stage of Wesley's abandonment of mysticism took place in May of that year. Under the influence of Peter Böhler, a Moravian, Wesley had been considering the doctrine of justification by faith.[23] This provided a foundation for assurance of salvation, which was precisely the thing Wesley had been seeking in his mystic exercises.[24] Slowly, he began to realize that the foundational issue was the atonement; the mystics Wesley read were silent on the reconciliation with God provided by Christ's atoning sacrifice, and tacitly

17. Wesley to Ann Bolton, April 24, 1777, 261–62.
18. Tuttle, *Mysticism*, 99.
19. Wesley, *Works* (Bicentennial) 18:213n95.
20. Wesley, *Works* (Bicentennial) 18:213n95.
21. Wesley, *Works* (Bicentennial) 18:213n95.
22. Wesley, *Works* (Bicentennial) 18:213n95.
23. Tuttle, *Mysticism*, 105.
24. Tuttle, *Mysticism*, 107–8.

endorsed a works-righteousness that focused on interior works of meditation and contemplation.[25] Years later, he explains his rejection of the mystics: "The chief of them do not appear to me to have any conception of church communion. Again, they slight not only works of piety, the ordinances of God, but even works of mercy. And yet most of them, yea, all that I have seen, hold justification by works. In general, they are 'wise above what is written,' indulging themselves in many unscriptural speculations."[26]

These "unscriptural speculations" clearly bothered Wesley, because he came back to it several times in later years. He writes to a friend: "In one point only our friends at Bristol have been once and again in some danger . . . of being a little hurt by reading those that are called Mystic authors. These (Madame Guyon in particular) have abundance of excellent sayings. They have many fine and elegant observations; but in the meantime they are immeasurably wise above that is written."[27] Evidently, the situation lay heavily on him; just two days later, he writes someone else, "You cannot imagine what trouble I have had for many years to prevent our friends from *refining* upon religion. Therefore I have industriously guarded them from meddling with the Mystic writers, as they are usually called; because these are the most artful refiners of it that ever appeared in the Christian world, and the most bewitching."[28] Wesley acknowledges here the powerful draw the mystics exerted on him. He writes this not as an external observer, but as a former participant. He continues, "There is something like enchantment in them. When you get into them, you know not how to get out. Some of the chief of these, though in different ways, are Jacob Behmen and Madame Guyon. My dear friend, come not into their secret; keep in the plain, open Bible way."[29] Wesley singled out Madame Guyon, especially; possibly because he considers her most dangerous, but more probably because she was the most popular of the mystics among the people to whom Wesley ministered. "Madame Guyon was a good woman and is a fine writer, but very far from judicious. Her writings will lead any one who is fond of them into unscriptural Quietism. They strike at the root, and tend to make us rest contented without either faith or works."[30]

25. Tuttle, *Mysticism*, 116–17.
26. Wesley, *Works* (Jackson) 3:160 (February 5, 1764).
27. Wesley to Penelope Newman, October 23, 1772, 341–42.
28. Wesley to Ann Bolton, October 25, 1772, 342.
29. Wesley to Ann Bolton, October 25, 1772, 342.
30. Wesley to Mary Bishop, September 19, 1773, 44.

In contrast, Wesley often explains his rejection of the mystics in terms of faithfulness to Scripture: "My censure of the Mystics is . . . owing . . . to my reverence for the Oracles of God, which, while I was fond of them, I regarded less and less; till, at length, finding I could not follow both, I exchanged the Mystic writers for the scriptural."[31] "But I found at length an absolute necessity of giving up either them or the Bible."[32] Not long after Wesley recognized the works-righteousness of the mystics for what it was, he had his famous heartwarming experience at Aldersgate, where he experienced justification by faith.

Opposition to Moravian Quietism

From this point on, Wesley distanced himself from mysticism, especially those aspects of it that focused on Quietism, the abandonment of the means of grace. This included breaking with the Moravian movement itself, which had initially helped him to see the flaws in mysticism and introduced him to the doctrine of justification by faith. When the question came to the means of grace, however, Wesley could not in good conscience give them up or continue to associate with those who did.

Wesley had initially been enamored of the Moravian movement and decided to journey to Germany shortly after his Aldersgate experience on May 24, 1738.[33] He sailed from England by June 14,[34] and arrived in Rotterdam the next day. He spent several days visiting Christians (and meeting Peter Böhler's father), and arrived on July 4 at Marienborn Castle, the home of Count Zinzendorf, the leader of the Moravians. After staying with him for a week and a half, Wesley traveled east to the main Moravian settlement at Herrnhut, arriving there on the first of August. Virtually everything he recorded of this trip was positive. In his journal, Wesley copied down *An Extract of the Constitution of the Church of the Moravian Brethren at Herrnhut, Laid before the Theological Order at Württemberg in the Year 1733*. In it is an account of the founding of the Moravian continual prayer meeting, which by the time Wesley arrived, had been going unbroken for over a decade:

---

31. Wesley, *Works* (Jackson) 3:19 (September 16, 1760).
32. Wesley to the Rev. Thomas Hartley, March 27, 1764, 234.
33. Wesley, *Works* (Jackson) 1:106 (June 7, 1738).
34. Wesley, *Works* (Jackson) 1:106–7 (June 14, 1738).

> In the year 1727, four-and-twenty men, and as many women, agreed that each of them would spend an hour in every day in praying to God for his blessing on his people; And for this purpose both the men and women chose a place where any of their own sex, who were in distress, might be present with them. The same number of unmarried women, of unmarried men, of boys, and of girls, were afterwards, at their desire, added to them; who pour out their souls before God, not only for their brethren, but also for other churches and persons, that have desired to be mentioned in their prayers. And this perpetual intercession has never ceased day or night, since its first beginning.[35]

This account is striking, especially insofar as it demonstrates a community commitment to regulated, disciplined, unified prayer, which one would think to be the antithesis of Quietism. And yet, although Wesley returned to England in high spirits, it was not to last. Quietism would soon raise its head in the small congregation of Moravian believers in the Fetter Lane society.

Little more than a year later, in November of 1739, some members of the Fetter Lane Society (which Wesley attended) began to take Quietist doctrinal positions. Shortly before that, a traveling Moravian minister named Philipp Molther had joined the group, since he was stranded in London for several months waiting for a boat.[36] He began to teach his Quietist doctrines, and soon some of the members stopped taking the Lord's Supper. They asserted that one who did not have the assurance of faith should "abstain from the means of grace, as they are called; the Lord's Supper in particular"[37] and wait in stillness until such faith was sovereignly gifted by God. Moreover, they "strongly intimated that none of them had any true faith."[38]

From Wesley's perspective, this was an absolute disaster. Assurance of salvation and the means of grace were two critical points of his doctrine. The end result was that "many of those who once knew in whom they had believed, were thrown into idle reasonings, and thereby filled with doubts and fears, from which they now found no way to escape."[39] After nearly two months of argumentation and attempts to persuade the

35. Wesley, *Works* (Jackson) 1:144 (August 10, 1738).
36. Wesley, *Works* (Bicentennial) 19:119n2.
37. Wesley, *Works* (Jackson) 1:247 (November 4, 1739).
38. Wesley, *Works* (Jackson) 1:247 (November 4, 1739).
39. Wesley, *Works* (Jackson) 1:248 (November 7, 1739).

Fetter Lane Society away from Quietism, Wesley had a long conversation with Molther. This was to no avail; when Wesley returned, he drew up a document clearly outlining the differences between himself and Molther; among them, that, "as to the way of faith, you [Moravians] believe... not to use so much private prayer."[40]

The following spring, the situation had worsened, and the followers of Molther were strongly urging people "not to go to church; not to communicate [i.e., take the Lord's Supper]; not to search the Scripture; not to use private prayer; at least, not so much, or not vocally, or not at any stated times."[41] Both John Wesley and his brother Charles again spoke to Molther, but nothing changed. Within a few months, John Wesley and those who held to his position withdrew from the Fetter Lane Society.

Eventually, John Wesley wrote to Count Zinzendorf in an attempt to straighten things out theologically. Zinzendorf's response absolutely dismissed Wesley's concerns and fully embraced Quietism. Zinzendorf writes, "We reject all self-denial. We trample upon it. We do, as believers, whatsoever we will, and nothing more. We laugh at all mortification. No purification precedes perfect love."[42] Wesley's break with the Moravians was permanent.

Abiding Influence

Despite his break with the mystic writers, Wesley continued to recommend them to his preachers from time to time, and he adapted the writings and lives of many mystics in his *Christian Library*. The continuing mystical influence can be seen, especially in his doctrines of Christian perfection and unceasing prayer. However, the differences, especially in the area of activity and Quietism, should be noted as well.

Wesley owed practically his whole idea of Christian perfection to the early writers who influenced him: Jeremy Taylor, Thomas à Kempis, and William Law. Tuttle concludes that "most of the basic characteristics of Wesley's doctrine find parallel consideration among those mystics whom he was reading while his ideas on perfection were first being formulated."[43] The ethical character of Christian perfection was not affected by Wesley's

---

40. Wesley, *Works* (Jackson) 1:257 (December 31, 1739).
41. Wesley, *Works* (Jackson) 1:269 (April 23, 1740).
42. Quoted in Moore, *Life*, 282–83.
43. Tuttle, *Mysticism*, 149.

break with Quietist forms of mysticism in the years following his experience on Aldersgate.[44]

Wesley's doctrine of prayer, especially unceasing prayer, was also initially influenced by the mystics. Although he criticized them for "disparaging prayer," later in his life he developed the idea of prayer as a "disposition of the heart" in a clearly mystical sense.[45] Tuttle notes, "Wesley singles out [mystical writers] Lopez and Brother Lawrence in particular for their practice of prayer as an uninterrupted communion—the practical result of praying without ceasing."[46] Nevertheless, Tuttle concludes, Wesley still "strongly discouraged the practice of wordless contemplation and mental prayer."[47] Perhaps the balance is best expressed in his advice to Ann Bolton: "There is no exercise more profitable to the soul than that of the presence of God. It is likewise of great use constantly and invariably to attend to His inward voice. And yet there is a danger even in this . . . it is very possible . . . that you may insensibly slide into Quietism, [and] may become less zealous of good works."[48]

Conclusion

The mystical ideal of the union with God, while enticing to Wesley, proved to be ultimately an illusion. While he always admired the personal sanctity of the mystics, he realized that their theology was fundamentally flawed: they rejected the means of grace, they conceived of a dark night of the soul that did not accord with the witness of Scripture, and they had a faulty (or nonexistent) doctrine of the atonement. Wesley eventually abandoned mystic Quietism for evangelical religion. Although the Moravians had been the ones who introduced Wesley to this evangelical religion, they eventually embraced Quietism as well. Wesley tried many times to convince them otherwise, but ultimately had to part ways with them. Wesley was to find the true goal of the Christian life in the unceasing prayer of Christian perfection.

---

44. Tuttle, *Mysticism*, 148.
45. Tuttle, *Mysticism*, 157.
46. Tuttle, *Mysticism*, 157.
47. Tuttle, *Mysticism*, 158.
48. Wesley to Ann Bolton, October 1, 1774, 115.

— 12 —

Prayer and Christian Perfection

SANCTIFICATION IS THE ONE area of John Wesley's theology that has probably been most subject to interest, scrutiny, and debate, and his doctrine of Christian perfection is doubtless the most controversial aspect within that area. Nevertheless, it is impossible to consider Wesley's understanding of prayer as the goal of the Christian life apart from his understanding of Christian perfection. Thankfully, in response to numerous misunderstandings and accusations, Wesley published his book *A Plain Account of Christian Perfection*, which clarifies many points. A full examination of this doctrine is outside the scope of this book, but this chapter presents a brief overview, to provide context for the further examination of unceasing prayer. Next, it looks at the role of prayer in Christian perfection, especially prayer's role in preserving it. Finally, it explores the expression of Christian perfection in unceasing prayer.

Understanding Christian Perfection

In answer to the question, "What is Christian perfection?" Wesley writes, "The loving [of] God with all our heart, mind, soul, and strength. This implies, that no wrong temper, none contrary to love, remains in the soul;

and that all the thoughts, words, and actions, are governed by pure love."[1] Elsewhere, he elaborates, saying that

> it is purity of intention, dedicating all the life to God. It is the giving God all our heart; it is one desire and design ruling all our tempers. It is the devoting, not a part, but all our soul, body, and substance to God. In another view, it is all the mind which was in Christ, enabling us to walk as Christ walked. It is the circumcision of the heart from all filthiness, all inward as well as outward pollution. It is a renewal of the heart in the whole image of God, the full likeness of Him that created it. In yet another, it is the loving God with all our heart, and our neighbour as ourselves.[2]

Wesley was, however, very careful to limit his definition of perfection. In speaking of those who had achieved Christian perfection, Wesley cautions that they "are not perfect in knowledge. They are not free from ignorance, no, nor from mistake. We are no more to expect any living man to be infallible, than to be omniscient. They are not free from infirmities, such as weakness or slowness of understanding, irregular quickness or heaviness of imagination . . . to which one might add a thousand nameless defects. . . . From such infirmities as these none are perfectly freed till their spirits return to God."[3] Wesley was challenged several times on this point and had to explain himself more fully. It seemed to many that he was contradicting himself. Wesley responded that he did not expect to be delivered from natural human mistakes "till this mortal puts on immortality. I believe this to be a natural consequence of the soul's dwelling in flesh and blood. For we cannot now think at all, but by the mediation of those bodily organs which have suffered equally with the rest of our frame. And hence we cannot avoid sometimes thinking wrong, till this corruptible shall have put on incorruption."[4]

The greatest controversy, though, was over the nature of sin in the believer, and over whether Christian perfection meant "sinless perfection." If this was the case, would it not mean that the Christian no longer needed the atoning work of Christ? Wesley explains that "the best of men still need Christ in his priestly office, to atone for their omissions, their short-comings, . . . their mistakes in judgment and practice, and their

1. Wesley, *Plain Account*, 394.
2. Wesley, *Plain Account*, 444.
3. Wesley, *Plain Account*, 374.
4. Wesley, *Plain Account*, 394.

defects of various kinds. For these are all deviations from the perfect law, and consequently need an atonement. Yet . . . they are not properly sins."[5] He argues this from Rom 13:10: "He that loveth, hath fulfilled the law; for love is the fulfilling of the law." If love was the fulfilling of the law, then the Christian that loved God fully, according to his or her own capacity, was fulfilling the law in a way that precluded sin.

Part of the controversy was how exactly Wesley defined sin. He defined it as "a voluntary transgression of a known law."[6] Wesley explains, "Now, mistakes, and whatever infirmities necessarily flow from the corruptible state of the body, are noway contrary to love; nor therefore, in the Scripture sense, sin. . . . Not only sin, properly so called, . . . but sin, improperly so called, (that is, an involuntary transgression of a divine law, known or unknown,) needs the atoning blood."[7] Therefore, Wesley understood his conception of Christian perfection not only to be biblical, but to affirm rather than undermine the atoning work of Christ. Wesley affirms that "there is no such perfection in this life as excludes these involuntary transgressions which I apprehend to be naturally consequent on the ignorance and mistakes inseparable from mortality . . . [and so, t]herefore, *sinless perfection* is a phrase I never use, lest I should seem to contradict myself."[8] To put an end to the matter, he concludes, "I believe, a person filled with the love of God is still liable to these involuntary transgressions. . . . Such transgressions you may call sins, if you please: I do not, for the reasons above-mentioned."[9]

These definitions of sin and perfection naturally lead to a couple of conclusions, which Wesley freely affirmed. First, if perfection does not apply to the limitations of flesh, then a Christian who was considered perfect, loving God completely, could still grow in knowledge and capacity for love. In response to the question, "Can those who are perfect grow in grace?" Wesley replies, "Undoubtedly they can; and that not only while they are in the body, but to all eternity."[10] Second, perfection does not eliminate the possibility of sin; that is, perfection is a state that must be diligently maintained. Wesley describes the watchfulness of these saints: "While they 'rejoice evermore, pray without ceasing, and in everything give thanks,' they

---

5. Wesley, *Plain Account*, 396.
6. Wesley, *Plain Account*, 396.
7. Wesley, *Plain Account*, 396.
8. Wesley, *Plain Account*, 396.
9. Wesley, *Plain Account*, 396.
10. Wesley, *Plain Account*, 426.

pray in particular, that they may never cease to watch, to deny themselves, to take up their cross daily, to fight the good fight of faith; and against the world, the devil, and their own manifold infirmities, till they are able to 'comprehend, with all saints, what is the length, and breadth, and height, and depth, and to know that love of Christ which passeth knowledge;' yea, to 'be filled with all the fulness of God.'"[11]

Prayer and Christian Perfection

Although all of the means of grace play a role in achieving Christian perfection in Wesley's scheme, he highlights the role of prayer: "If our ultimate end is the love of God, to which the several particular Christian virtues lead us, so the means leading to these are to communicate every possible time, and, whatsoever we do, to pray without ceasing; not to be content with our solemn devotions, whether public or private, but at all times and in all places to make fervent returns 'by ejaculations' and 'abrupt intercourses of the mind with God'; to thrust 'these between all our other employments,' if it be only by a word, a thought, a look."[12] In a letter to Mary Bishop concerned with sanctification, he advises her, "Your continual prayer should be for faith and love."[13]

Wesley characterizes the attainment of entire sanctification as God's answer to prayer: "Nay, it is true still farther that many serious, humble, sober-minded believers, who do feel the love of God sometimes, and do then rejoice in God their Saviour, cannot be content with this; but pray continually, that he would enable them to love, and 'rejoice in the Lord always.' And no fact under heaven is more undeniable, than that God does answer this prayer."[14] In the case of a woman who received entire sanctification a week after receiving pardon for sin, he writes, "We had a remarkable instance of God's hearing prayer."[15]

Since sanctification is an act of God in answer to prayer, then the responsibility of believers is clear: "It is therefore undoubtedly our duty to pray and look for full salvation every day, every hour, every moment, without waiting till we have either done or suffered more. Why should not

---

11. Wesley, "Sermon 110," 237–38.
12. Wesley to Anne Granville, December 12, 1730, 66.
13. Wesley to Mary Bishop, November 27, 1770, 209.
14. Wesley, *Works* (Jackson) 3:341 (August 27, 1768).
15. Wesley, *Works* (Jackson) 3:477 (August 7, 1772).

this be the accepted time?"[16] Wesley's advice always carried the optimistic tone that one should expect God to answer the prayer for sanctification, and soon: "Continue instant in prayer; and watch against whatever you know by experience to be a weight upon your mind. . . . How soon may your heart be all love!"[17]

Preserving Christian Perfection

Attaining Christian perfection is no mean feat. Preserving it requires constant vigilance; it is practically impossible to maintain in a static state, as Wesley writes: "In every state of mind, in that of conviction or justification or sanctification, I believe every person may either go sensibly backward, or seem to stand still, or go forward. I incline to think all the persons you mention were fully sanctified. But some of them, watching unto prayer, went on from faith to faith; while the others, being less watchful, seemed to stand still, but were indeed imperceptibly backsliding."[18] In writing about the witness of sanctification, Wesley comments that there are circumstances in which a person can lose it: "Indeed, they cannot retain it in two cases: either if they do not continue steadily watching unto prayer; or, secondly, if they give way to reasoning, if they let go any part of 'love's divine simplicity.'"[19]

This is not only true of those who have reached the heights of Christian perfection, but of those who are somewhere on the way; the further they have progressed, the more important vigilance becomes in preserving it, as Wesley describes: "Hence, it is impossible that any should retain what they receive, without improving it. Add to this, that the more we have received, the more of care and labour is required, the more watchfulness and prayer, the more circumspection and earnestness in all manner of conversation. Is it any wonder, then, that they who forget this, should soon lose what they had received? Nay, who were *taught* to forget it? Not to watch! Not to pray,—under the pretence of praying always!"[20] Wesley himself felt the struggle keenly and sympathized with those whose mundane duties dominated their time. In a letter to Ebenezer Blackwell, he writes: "I find the engaging, though but a little, in these temporal affairs, is apt to damp and

16. Wesley to Miss March, June 27, 1760, 100.
17. Wesley to Jane Hilton, June 25, 1768, 94.
18. Wesley to Elizabeth Ritchie, January 19, 1782, 103.
19. Wesley to Peggy Dale, January 30, 1768, 78.
20. Wesley, *Works* (Jackson) 3:204 (January 31, 1765).

deaden the soul; and there is no remedy but continual prayer. What, then, but the mighty power of God can keep your soul alive, who are engaged all the day long in such a multiplicity of them? It is well that His grace is sufficient for you. But do you not find need to pray always?"[21]

Despite Wesley's warnings and advice, many people who appeared to have reached Christian perfection eventually fell back from it: "Hardly three in five of those that are either justified or sanctified keep the gift of God a year to an end. So much the more exhort them to watch and pray that they enter not into temptation."[22] The end result was that there were many who thought they had attained Christian perfection, but backslid. Many of them questioned whether it was gone past hope of recovery, or if there was mercy for second chances. Wesley decidedly taught that God was always ready to show mercy to those who aspired to perfect love. "Nothing is more certain than that God is willing to give always what He gives once. If, therefore, He now gives you power to yield Him your whole heart, you may confidently expect the continuance of that power till your spirit returns to God, provided you continue watching unto prayer, denying yourself, and taking up your cross daily."[23] In a letter to Philothea Briggs, a backslidden pursuer of entire sanctification, Wesley writes encouragingly: "You did yourself enjoy a foretaste of that constant communion with God, though it did not continue long. And you know it was given you in a moment. It was the same case with Sally Ryan, with Nancy Bolton, and with all those whom I have known that are now enabled to pray without ceasing. To every one of them that blessing was given in an instant. So it will be given to *you* again."[24]

Christian Perfection and Unceasing Prayer

Many times, Wesley uses the Thessalonian trifecta of "rejoicing always, praying without ceasing, and giving thanks in all things" as his litmus test and shorthand for Christian perfection. In his sermon "The Scripture Way of Salvation" Wesley poses the question, "But what is perfection?" and gives the answer, "It is love 'rejoicing evermore, praying without ceasing, in everything giving thanks.'"[25] Over and over throughout his *Plain Ac-*

21. Wesley to Ebenezer Blackwell, March 15, 1748, 131.
22. Wesley to Hannah Ball, August 14, 1771, 273.
23. Wesley to Mrs. Crosby, January 1, 1770, 171.
24. Wesley to Philothea Briggs, September 29, 1773, 45.
25. Wesley, "Sermon 43," 46.

count of Christian Perfection, he equated this trio with Christian perfection. He writes, "The perfection I hold [is], 'Love rejoicing evermore, praying without ceasing, and in every thing giving thanks.'"[26] In response to the question, "Does then Christian perfection imply any more than sincerity?" Wesley answers, "Not if you mean by that word, love filling the heart, expelling pride, anger, desire, self-will; rejoicing evermore, praying without ceasing, and in everything giving thanks."[27]

Later in the book, he writes, "[Christian perfection] is 'perfect love.'... This is the essence of it; its properties, or inseparable fruits, are, rejoicing evermore, praying without ceasing, and in everything giving thanks ... [and entirely sanctified Christians] enjoy perfect love; they feel this, and this alone; they 'rejoice evermore, pray without ceasing, and in everything give thanks.' Now, this is all that I mean by perfection; therefore, these are witnesses of the perfection which I preach."[28]

There is an organic connection between these three activities, which Wesley explains in his *Notes*: "*Rejoice evermore*—In uninterrupted happiness in God; *pray without ceasing*—Which is the fruit of always rejoicing in the Lord; *in everything give thanks*—Which is the fruit of both the former."[29] In other words, each of the three builds on the previous ones; the earlier ones lead to the later ones. Although in some sense a progression, one must not ignore the fundamental unity of these three. Wesley continues, "Prayer may be said to be the breath of our spiritual life. He that lives cannot possibly cease breathing. So much as we really enjoy of the presence of God, so much prayer and praise do we offer up without ceasing; else our rejoicing is but delusion. Thanksgiving is inseparable from true prayer: it is almost essentially connected with it."[30] If praying is like breathing, then the one who does not pray unceasingly is not yet spiritually alive in the fullest sense. If praying without ceasing is the fruit of rejoicing evermore, then rejoicing that fails to lead to unceasing prayer is delusion, and one has failed to "really enjoy the presence of God." Finally, Wesley concludes, "He that always prays is ever giving praise, whether in ease or pain, both for prosperity and for the greatest adversity."[31] Therefore, in examining

26. Wesley, *Plain Account*, 418.
27. Wesley, *Plain Account*, 418.
28. Wesley, *Plain Account*, 442.
29. Wesley, *Explanatory Notes*, 531.
30. Wesley, *Explanatory Notes*, 531.
31. Wesley, *Explanatory Notes*, 531.

prayer, especially unceasing prayer, in the theology of Wesley, one must not introduce artificial distinctions that Wesley himself would have rejected. The focus of this book is prayer, but unceasing prayer overlaps rejoicing and thanksgiving in the writings of Wesley, and the three should be examined together whenever they occur together.

As can be seen, Wesley's understanding of Christian perfection included prayer without ceasing, making prayer more than just a means to an end. Wesley saw that prayer was not only the means, but also a goal of holiness. The importance of this should not be underestimated. Not only does this show Wesley's conception of Christian perfection to be fully active, even apart from social action (in contrast to more passive, Quietist views, a feature examined more closely in the previous chapter), but Wesley saw the activity of prayer, not just as building toward eventual perfection, but as actually partaking of it.

In *The Character of a Methodist*, Wesley presents the concept of praying without ceasing as a quality he expected all good Methodists to exhibit:

> For indeed he "prays without ceasing." It is given him "always to pray, and not to faint." Not that he is always in the house of prayer; though he neglects no opportunity of being there. Neither is he always on his knees, although he often is, or on his face, before the Lord his God. Nor yet is he always crying aloud to God, or calling upon him in words: For many times "the Spirit maketh intercession for him with groans that cannot be uttered." But at all times the language of his heart is this: "Thou brightness of the eternal glory, unto thee is my heart, though without a voice, and my silence speaketh unto thee." And this is true prayer, and this alone. But his heart is ever lifted up to God, at all times and in all places. In this he is never hindered, much less interrupted, by any person or thing. In retirement or company, in leisure, business, or conversation, his heart is ever with the Lord. Whether he lie down or rise up, God is in all his thoughts; he walks with God continually, having the loving eye of his mind still fixed upon him, and everywhere "seeing him that is invisible."[32]

Wesley writes to Philothea Briggs, "Your continual prayer should be, 'Lord, increase my faith!' A continual desire is a continual prayer—that is, in a low sense of the word; for there is a far higher sense, such an open intercourse with God, such a close, uninterrupted communion with him,

---

32. Wesley, *Character of a Methodist*, 343.

as Gregory Lopez experienced, and not a few of our brethren and sisters now alive."[33]

In short, Wesley's conception of unceasing prayer was broad enough that he felt it could be done in any sort of life: "No business, therefore, of any kind, no conversation, need hinder one that is strong in faith from rejoicing evermore, praying without ceasing, and in everything giving thanks."[34] Yet even if this kind of prayer was not easily attainable for someone, he took it, as he writes to Ebenezer Blackwell, as pointing to a greater need to set aside time for formal prayer: "And if you can't always say, 'My hands are but employed below; / My heart is still with Thee,' is there not the more occasion for some season of solemn retirement (if it were possible, every day) wherein you may withdraw your mind from earth, and even the accounts between God and your own soul?"[35]

In examining Wesley's idea of unceasing prayer in relation to Christian perfection, one is bound to notice a resemblance to certain mystical writings. In particular, the idea that prayer was primarily a "disposition of the heart" recalls a number of Catholic mystic writers.[36] Gregory Lopez, mentioned above, was a sixteenth-century Spanish Catholic mystic. In fact, the very term *Christian perfection* is the title of a book by Francis Fenelon, a well-known Catholic mystic writer of the late seventeenth century. However, Wesley's conception of prayer without ceasing should be carefully distinguished from Quietist forms of unceasing prayer, which Wesley strongly rejected.[37] While Wesley's attitude toward Christian mysticism varied during his life, he ultimately denounced passivity in both prayer and holiness. Wesley's understanding of unceasing prayer was, in the end, the loving desire to please God, and this absolutely had an active component.

Wesley took seriously the position of 1 Thess 5:17 as Paul's command to the people of God. Unceasing prayer is not an optional part of the Christian life, a novel exercise for those bored with the other means of grace, but an intrinsic part of the Christian's duty to God. "Beware, then, thou who art called by the name of Christ, that thou come not short of the mark of thy high calling," writes Wesley. "Thou shalt 'rejoice evermore;' thou shalt 'pray without ceasing;' thou shalt 'in everything give thanks.' Thou shalt do the will of God

---

33. Wesley to Philothea Briggs, October 16, 1771, 283.
34. Wesley to Philothea Briggs, August 31, 1772, 338.
35. Wesley to Ebenezer Blackwell, March 15, 1748, 131.
36. Tuttle, *Mysticism*, 157.
37. See previous chapter of this book.

PRAYER AND CHRISTIAN PERFECTION

on earth as it is done in heaven."[38] In rejecting salvation by works, Wesley confronted those who would establish their own righteousness, saying, "Are you able to 'love God with all your heart?' to love all mankind as your own soul? to 'pray without ceasing? in every thing to give thanks?' to have God always before you? and to keep every affection, desire, and thought, in obedience to his law?"[39] It is clear that not only did Wesley view unceasing prayer as a means of holiness and a goal of holiness, but as a duty and responsibility, and to neglect or abandon this duty constitutes sin.

This duty should not be thought of as burdensome. Wesley was also comfortable using this verse as a promise, to encourage the family of God and inspire them to further holiness. "We may yet farther observe, that every command in holy writ is only a covered promise. . . . Does he command us then to 'pray without ceasing?' to 'rejoice evermore?' to be 'holy as He is holy?' It is enough: He will work in us this very thing: It shall be unto us according to his word."[40] At the root, Wesley looks to God's character and promises, faithfully trusting that God will work these things in the lives of Christians even as they endeavor to obey God. "He will lead you forth beside the waters of comfort, and keep you every moment: So that loving him with all your heart, (which is the sum of all perfection,) you will 'rejoice evermore, pray without ceasing, and in everything give thanks,' till 'an abundant entrance is ministered unto you into his everlasting kingdom!'"[41]

Naturally, Wesley encountered many who hesitated to affirm that such a state could be achieved. In response to this view, Wesley argues, "[Paul,] after exhorting the Christians at Thessalonica, and in them all Christians in all ages, to 'rejoice evermore, pray without ceasing, and in everything give thanks,'—immediately adds, (as if on purpose to answer those who denied, not the *power*, but the *will* of God to work this in them,) 'For this is the will of God concerning you in Christ Jesus.'"[42]

How then could this promise be effected in the life of the believer? Wesley knew it would require supernatural power, saying, "We trust to love the Lord our God, not only as we do now, with a weak, though sincere affection, but 'with all our heart, with all our mind, with all our soul, and with all our strength.' We look for power to 'rejoice evermore, to pray without

38. Wesley, "Sermon 9," 110–11.
39. Wesley, "Sermon 6," 71–72.
40. Wesley, "Sermon 25," 314.
41. Wesley, "Sermon 83," 492.
42. Wesley, "Sermon 76," 420.

ceasing, and in everything to give thanks;' knowing, 'this is the will of God in Christ Jesus concerning us.'"[43]

Wesley found the power for completion of the work of sanctification in the same power that began the work: the love of God. "It is by faith that the eye of the mind is opened, to see the light of the glorious love of God: And as long as it is steadily fixed thereon . . . we are more and more filled with the love of God and man; with meekness, gentleness, longsuffering; with all the fruits of holiness which are through Christ Jesus, to the glory of God the Father."[44] The one who is fully focused on this love "walketh in the light as God is in the light, rejoicing evermore, praying without ceasing, and in every thing giving thanks; enjoying whatever is the will of God concerning him in Christ Jesus."[45] Because of this, Wesley's advice to those not yet fully sanctified is not to "try harder," but to practice an awareness of the constant love of God. Perpetually perceiving this love is an almost inevitable route to sanctification. Wesley says, "When thy whole soul is full of this light, thou wilt be able . . . to 'rejoice evermore, to pray without ceasing, and in everything to give thanks.' For who can be constantly sensible of the loving presence of God without 'rejoicing evermore?' Who can have the loving eye of his soul perpetually fixed upon God, but he will 'pray without ceasing?'"[46]

The ultimate question, though, is how does one recognize that one has attained this level of Christian perfection? Wesley answers that one may feel confident one has attained Christian perfection, "[w]hen, after having been fully convinced of inbred sin, by a far deeper and clearer conviction than that he experienced before justification, and after having experienced a gradual mortification of it, he experiences a total death to sin, and an entire renewal in the love and image of God, so as to rejoice evermore, to pray without ceasing, and 'in everything to give thanks.'"[47]

In several places, Wesley offers descriptions of those who had attained Christian perfection. The perfect Christian "'prays without ceasing;' at all times the language of his heart is this, 'Unto thee is my mouth, though without a voice, and my silence speaketh unto thee.' His heart is lifted up to God at all times, and in all places. . . . Whether he lie down,

---

43. Wesley, "Sermon 42," 33.
44. Wesley, "Sermon 28," 363.
45. Wesley, "Sermon 28," 363.
46. Wesley, "Sermon 118," 298–99.
47. Wesley, *Plain Account*, 400.

or rise up, 'God is in all his thoughts:' He walks with God continually; having the loving eye of his soul fixed on him, and everywhere 'seeing Him that is invisible.'"[48] Wesley describes those whom he knew that loved God wholeheartedly: "[God] is their one desire, their one delight, and they are continually happy in him. . . . They feel as sincere, fervent, constant a desire for the happiness of every man, good or bad, friend or enemy, as for their own. They rejoice evermore, pray without ceasing, and in everything give thanks. Their souls are continually streaming up to God, in holy joy, prayer, and praise."[49] As has been shown, prayer is a central element in sanctification, and unceasing prayer is a primary identifying marker of Christian perfection. Not only is it commanded, but it is promised, and that promise is fulfilled through God's transforming love, enabling the Christian to live a life of full devotion and unceasing prayer.

---

48. Wesley, *Plain Account*, 371.
49. Wesley, *Plain Account*, 418.

Bibliography

Baker, Frank. *John Wesley and the Church of England*. Nashville: Abingdon, 1970.
Boice, James Montgomery. *Whatever Happened to the Gospel of Grace?* Grand Rapids: Crossway, 2001.
Brooks, Thomas. "The Privy Key of Heaven." In vol. 2 of *The Complete Works of Thomas Brooks*, edited by Alexander B. Grosart, 139–299. Carlisle, PA: Banner of Truth Trust, 1980.
Calvin, John. *Institutes of the Christian Religion*. Translated by Ford Lewis Battles. Louisville: Westminster John Knox, 2006.
Church of England. "Articles of Religion." https://www.churchofengland.org/prayer-and-worship/worship-texts-and-resources/book-common-prayer/articles-religion#I.
Clapper, George S. *John Wesley on Religious Affections*. Metuchen, NJ: Scarecrow, 1989.
Clarke, Adam. *Memoirs of the Wesley Family*. 4th ed. New York: Carlton & Porter, 1859.
Collins, Kenneth J. *The Theology of John Wesley*. Nashville: Abingdon, 2007.
Davies, Horton. *Worship and Theology in England: From Watts and Wesley to Maurice, 1690–1850*. Princeton: Princeton University Press, 1961.
Fenelon, Francois. "On Simplicity." In *Selections from the Writings of Fenelon*, 130–37. Boston: Hilliard, 1831.
Heitzenrater, Richard P. "Editorial Introduction." In *Works* (Bicentennial) 18:309.
Johnson, Steve. "John Wesley's Liturgical Theology." PhD diss., University of Manchester, 2016. https://pure.manchester.ac.uk/ws/portalfiles/portal/54581738/FULL_TEXT.PDF.
Jones, Abraham. Letter to John Wesley, December 12, 1742. In *John Wesley's In-Correspondence (1741–45)*, Wesley Works Editorial Project, 149–50. https://wesleyworks.wordpress.com/wp-content/uploads/2023/09/jw-in-correspondence-1741-45.pdf.
Knight, Henry H., III. *The Presence of God in the Christian Life: John Wesley and the Means of Grace*. Lanham, MD: Scarecrow, 1992.
Law, William. *A Practical Treatise upon Christian Perfection*. Edited by L. H. M. Soulsby. London: Longmans, 1901.
———. *A Serious Call to a Devout and Holy Life*. Grand Rapids: Eerdmans, 1966.
Lindström, Harald. *Wesley and Sanctification*. Grand Rapids: Francis Asbury, 1980.

BIBLIOGRAPHY

Marshall, Ed. "Queries." *Notes & Queries*, 5th ser., 6 (July–December 1876) 87.

Mohler, R. Albert, Jr. "'Evangelical': What's in a Name?" In *The Coming Evangelical Crisis: Current Challenges to the Authority of Scripture and the Gospel*, edited by John H. Armstrong, 29–44. Chicago: Moody, 1996.

Moore, Henry. *The Life of the Rev. John Wesley*. Vol. 1. New York: Bangs and Emory, 1826.

Oden, Thomas C. *John Wesley's Scriptural Christianity*. Grand Rapids: Zondervan, 1994.

Olson, Roger. "Arminianism Is God-Centered Theology." In *Grace for All: The Arminian Dynamics of Salvation*, edited by Clark H. Pinnock and John D. Wagner, 1–17. Eugene, OR: Resource, 2015.

Pendarves, Mary. Letter to John Wesley, August 26, 1731. In *John Wesley's In-Correspondence (1731–35)*, Wesley Works Editorial Project, 33. https://wesleyworks.wordpress.com/wp-content/uploads/2023/09/jw-in-correspondence-1731-35.pdf.

Ramsay, Chevalier. *The Philosophical Principles of Natural and Revealed Religion*. Glasgow: Foulis, 1749.

Selleck, J. Brian. "The Book of Common Prayer in the Theology of John Wesley." PhD diss., Drew University, 1983.

Starkey, Lycurgus M., Jr. *The Work of the Holy Spirit: A Study in Wesleyan Theology*. New York: Abingdon, 1962.

Taylor, Jeremy. *The Rule and Exercises of Holy Living*. London: Longmans, 1918.

Thomas à Kempis. *The Imitation of Christ*. Edited by Paul M. Bechtel. Chicago: Moody, 1980.

Tuttle, Robert G., Jr. *Mysticism in the Wesleyan Tradition*. Grand Rapids: Francis Asbury, 1989.

Wade, William Nash. "A History of Public Worship in the Methodist Episcopal Church, South, from 1784 to 1905." PhD diss., University of Notre Dame, 1981.

Wesley, Charles. Letter to John Wesley, January 5–22, 1729. In *John Wesley's In-Correspondence (1724–30)*, Wesley Works Editorial Project, 93–96. https://wesleyworks.wordpress.com/wp-content/uploads/2023/09/jw-in-correspondence-1724-30.pdf.

———. Letter to John Wesley, May 5, 1729. In *John Wesley's In-Correspondence (1724–30)*, Wesley Works Editorial Project, 97–99. https://wesleyworks.wordpress.com/wp-content/uploads/2023/09/jw-in-correspondence-1724-30.pdf.

Wesley, John. *The Bicentennial Edition of the Works of John Wesley*. Edited by Albert Outler, et al. 35 vols. Nashville: Abingdon, 1984–.

———. *The Character of a Methodist*. In *Works* (Jackson) 8:340–47.

———. *A Christian Library*. 1821 ed. 30 vols. Wesley Center Online. https://wesley.nnu.edu/john-wesley/a-christian-library/.

———. *A Collection of Forms of Prayer (1733)*. In *Works* (Jackson) 11:203–37.

———. *A Collection of Prayers for Families*. In *Works* (Jackson) 11:237–59.

———. *Explanatory Notes on the New Testament*. 12th ed. New York: Carlton & Porter, 1754.

———, ed. "An Extract from the *Whole Duty of Man*, Part IV–VIII." Wesley Center Online. http://wesley.nnu.edu/john-wesley/a-christian-library/a-christian-library-volume-12/an-extract-from-the-whole-duty-of-man-part-iv-viii/.

———. *A Farther Appeal to Men of Reason and Religion, Part I*. In *Works* (Jackson) 8:46–134.

———. *A Farther Appeal to Men of Reason and Religion, Part II*. In *Works* (Jackson) 8:136–200.

BIBLIOGRAPHY

———. *A Farther Appeal to Men of Reason and Religion, Part III.* In *Works* (Jackson) 8:201–47.

———. "Farther Thoughts on Separation from the Church." In *Works* (Jackson) 13:272–74.

———. "Hymn 159." In *Works* (Bicentennial) 7:279–80.

———. "Hymn 341." In *Works* (Bicentennial) 7:502–3.

———. "Hymn 363." In *Works* (Bicentennial) 7:532–33.

———. "Hymn 365." In *Works* (Bicentennial) 7:535.

———. "Hymn 516." In *Works* (Bicentennial) 7:708.

———. *John Wesley's Manuscript Prayer Manual.* Edited by Randy L. Maddox. Wesley Works Editorial Project, updated Jan. 29, 2018. https://wesleyworks.files.wordpress.com/2018/03/jw-ms-prayer-manual.pdf.

———. *The Journal of the Rev. John Wesley, A.M.* Edited by Nehemiah Curnock. Vol. 1. New York: Eaton & Mains, 1909.

———. Letter to Abraham Orchard, January 1, 1783. In *Letters* (Telford) 7:161.

———. Letter to Adam Clarke, July 2, 1786. In *Letters* (Telford) 7:335.

———. Letter to Adam Clarke, November 9, 1787. In *Letters* (Telford) 8:21–22.

———. Letter to Adam Clarke, November 21, 1787. In *Letters* (Telford) 8:22–23.

———. Letter to Adam Clarke, October 28, 1790. In *Letters* (Telford) 8:244.

———. Letter to Adam Clarke, October 31, 1789. In *Letters* (Telford) 8:182.

———. Letter to Adam Clarke, September 9, 1790. In *Letters* (Telford) 8:237.

———. Letter to a Friend, September 20, 1757. In *Letters* (Telford) 3:226–28.

———. Letter to Alexander Knox, June 5, 1778. In *Letters* (Telford) 6:314.

———. Letter to Ann Bolton, April 24, 1777. In *Letters* (Telford) 6:261–62.

———. Letter to Ann Bolton, August 25, 1771. In *Letters* (Telford) 5:275–76.

———. Letter to Ann Bolton, August 31, 1784. In *Letters* (Telford) 7:233.

———. Letter to Ann Bolton, December 28, 1771. In *Letters* (Telford) 5:295.

———. Letter to Ann Bolton, January 5, 1783. In *Letters* (Telford) 7:161–62.

———. Letter to Ann Bolton, June 28, 1784. In *Letters* (Telford) 7:223–24.

———. Letter to Ann Bolton, October 1, 1774. In *Letters* (Telford) 6:115–16.

———. Letter to Ann Bolton, October 25, 1772. In *Letters* (Telford) 5:342–43.

———. Letter to Ann Foard, August 21, 1766. In *Letters* (Telford) 5:25.

———. Letter to Ann Foard, December 2, 1767. In *Letters* (Telford) 5:68.

———. Letter to Ann Foard, January 15, 1767. In *Letters* (Telford) 5:37.

———. Letter to Ann Granville, December 12, 1730. In *Letters* (Telford) 1:66–67.

———. Letter to Ann Granville, October 3, 1731. In *Works* (Bicentennial), 25:317–20.

———. Letter to Ann Granville, September 27, 1730. In *Letters* (Telford) 1:53–56.

———. Letter to Ann Loxdale, July 14, 1781. In *Letters* (Telford) 7:73.

———. Letter to Ann Loxdale, July 24, 1782. In *Letters* (Telford) 7:130–31.

———. Letter to Ann Taylor, March 8, 1787. In *Letters* (Telford) 7:374.

———. Letter to a Roman Catholic. In *Works* (Jackson) 10:80–86.

———. Letter to Charles Wesley, March 17, 1788. In *Letters* (Telford) 8:45–46.

———. Letter to Charles Wesley, December 11, 1762. In *Letters* (Telford) 4:196–97.

———. Letter to Charles Wesley, July 31, 1747. In *Letters* (Telford) 2:108–9.

———. Letter to Damaris Perronet, March 30, 1771. In *Letters* (Telford) 5:233–35.

———. Letter to Dorothy Furly, October 21, 1757. In *Letters* (Telford) 3:230–31.

———. Letter to Dorothy Furly, September 25, 1757. In *Letters* (Telford) 3:228–29.

———. Letter to Dr. John Robertson, September 24, 1753. In *Letters* (Telford) 3:104–10.

———. Letter to Duncan McAllum, January 20, 1789. In *Letters* (Telford) 8:110.
———. Letter to the Earl of Dartmouth, June 14, 1775. In *Letters* (Telford) 6:155–60.
———. Letter to Ebenezer Blackwell, March 15, 1748. In *Letters* (Telford) 2:131.
———. Letter to Edward Jackson, October 24, 1788. In *Letters* (Telford) 8:98–99.
———. Letter to Elizabeth Ritchie, January 19, 1782. In *Letters* (Telford) 7:102–3.
———. Letter to Freeborn Garrettson, July 15, 1789. In *Letters* (Telford) 8:154.
———. Letter to George Cussons, November 18, 1768. In *Letters* (Telford) 5:112–13.
———. Letter to Hannah Ball, April 13, 1786. In *Letters* (Telford) 7:324–25.
———. Letter to Hannah Ball, August 14, 1771. In *Letters* (Telford) 5:272–73.
———. Letter to Harriet Lewis, April 2, 1789. In *Letters* (Telford) 8:127.
———. Letter to Henry Eames, July 15, 1789. In *Letters* (Telford) 8:153–54.
———. Letter to His Father, December 10, 1734. In *Letters* (Telford) 1:166–78.
———. Letter to James Currie, February 19, 1788. In *Letters* (Telford) 8:37.
———. Letter to James Hutton, August 15, 1739. In *Letters* (Telford) 1:332.
———. Letter to James Hutton, July 2, 1739. In *Letters* (Telford) 1:323–27.
———. Letter to James Hutton, May 7, 1739. In *Letters* (Telford) 1:304–7.
———. Letter to James Lowther, July 1, 1759. In *Letters* (Telford) 4:65–66.
———. Letter to Jane Hilton, June 25, 1768. In *Letters* (Telford) 5:94.
———. Letter to John Burton, October 10, 1735. In *Letters* (Telford) 1:188–91.
———. Letter to John Fletcher, March 20, 1768. In *Letters* (Telford) 5:82–85.
———. Letter to John Fletcher, March 22, 1771. In *Letters* (Telford) 5:231.
———. Letter to John Newton, May 14, 1765. In *Letters* (Telford) 4:297–300.
———. Letter to John Robson, September 30, 1735. In *Letters* (Telford) 1:183–84.
———. Letter to John Simpson, November 28, 1774. In *Letters* (Telford) 6:123–24.
———. Letter to John Trembath, August 17, 1760. In *Letters* (Telford) 4:102–3.
———. Letter to John Valton, November 12, 1771. In *Letters* (Telford) 5:289.
———. Letter to Joseph Benson, December 11, 1772. In *Letters* (Telford) 6:3.
———. Letter to Joseph Benson, November 30, 1770. In *Letters* (Telford) 5:211–12.
———. Letter to Joseph Taylor, September 9, 1782. In *Letters* (Telford) 7:138–39.
———. Letter to Joshua Keighley, February 19, 1787. In *Letters* (Telford) 7:370–71.
———. Letter to Mary Bishop, December 26, 1776. In *Letters* (Telford) 6:244–46.
———. Letter to Mary Bishop, March 8, 1771. In *Letters* (Telford) 5:227.
———. Letter to Mary Bishop, November 27, 1770. In *Letters* (Telford) 5:209–10.
———. Letter to Mary Bishop, September 19, 1773. In *Letters* (Telford) 6:43–44.
———. Letter to Mary Bosanquet, March 26, 1770. In *Letters* (Telford) 5:187.
———. Letter to Mary Cooke, December 14, 1785. In *Letters* (Telford) 7:303–4.
———. Letter to Mary Cooke, December 21, 1787. In *Letters* (Telford) 8:28.
———. Letter to Mary Stokes, January, 1772. In *Letters* (Telford) 5:302–3.
———. Letter to Miss Bishop, October 18, 1778. In *Letters* (Telford) 6:326–27.
———. Letter to Miss March, August 12, 1769. In *Letters* (Telford) 5:147–48.
———. Letter to Miss March, July 1, 1772. In *Letters* (Telford) 5:326.
———. Letter to Miss March, June 17, 1774. In *Letters* (Telford) 6:91–92.
———. Letter to Miss March, June 25, 1771. In *Letters* (Telford) 5:261–62.
———. Letter to Miss March, June 27, 1760. In *Letters* (Telford) 4:100–101.
———. Letter to Miss March, March 4, 1760. In *Letters* (Telford) 4:85–86.
———. Letter to Miss March, March 29, 1760. In *Letters* (Telford) 4:90.
———. Letter to Molly Wesley, November 24, 1759. In *Letters* (Telford) 4:79–80.
———. Letter to Mr. T. H., etc., December 12, 1760. In *Letters* (Telford) 4:119–24.

———. Letter to Mrs. Barton, April 9, 1769. In *Letters* (Telford) 5:131–32.
———. Letter to Mrs. Barton, November 5, 1770. In *Letters* (Telford) 5:206.
———. Letter to Mrs. Bennis, September 10, 1773. In *Letters* (Telford) 6:40.
———. Letter to Mrs. Cock, April 7, 1789. In *Letters* (Telford) 8:128.
———. Letter to Mrs. Crosby, January 1, 1770. In *Letters* (Telford) 5:171.
———. Letter to Mrs. Gair, November 5, 1774. In *Letters* (Telford) 6:117–18.
———. Letter to Mrs. Johnston, June 1, 1778. In *Letters* (Telford) 6:310–11.
———. Letter to Mrs. Knapp, March 25, 1781. In *Letters* (Telford) 7:52.
———. Letter to Mrs. Pendarves, August 12, 1731. In *Letters* (Telford) 1:101–3.
———. Letter to Mrs. Susanna Wesley, March 19, 1727. In *Letters* (Telford) 1:41–44.
———. Letter to Mrs. Susanna Wesley, May 28, 1725. In *Letters* (Telford) 1:15–17.
———. Letter to Mrs. Woodhouse, January 1, 1770. In *Letters* (Telford) 5:174.
———. Letter to Mrs. Woodhouse, May 17, 1766. In *Letters* (Telford) 5:11–12.
———. Letter to "Our Brethren in America," September 10, 1784. In *Letters* (Telford) 7:238–39.
———. Letter to Peggy Dale, January 30, 1768. In *Letters* (Telford) 5:78–79.
———. Letter to Penelope Newman, August 9, 1776. In *Letters* (Telford) 6:227.
———. Letter to Penelope Newman, October 23, 1772. In *Letters* (Telford) 5:341–42.
———. Letter to Peter Garforth, August 9, 1783. In *Letters* (Telford) 7:187.
———. Letter to Philothea Briggs, August 14, 1771. In *Letters* (Telford) 5:273–74.
———. Letter to Philothea Briggs, August 31, 1772. In *Letters* (Telford) 5:337–38.
———. Letter to Philothea Briggs, July 23, 1772. In *Letters* (Telford) 5:331.
———. Letter to Philothea Briggs, November 3, 1771. In *Letters* (Telford) 5:285–86.
———. Letter to Philothea Briggs, October 16, 1771. In *Letters* (Telford) 5:282–83.
———. Letter to Philothea Briggs, September 8, 1773. In *Letters* (Telford) 6:39.
———. Letter to Philothea Briggs, September 29, 1773. In *Letters* (Telford) 6:45.
———. Letter to Richard Rodda, January 17, 1787. In *Letters* (Telford) 7:364.
———. Letter to Robert Carr Brackenbury, July 9, 1781. In *Letters* (Telford) 8:274.
———. Letter to Robert Carr Brackenbury, November 24, 1785. In *Letters* (Telford) 7:301–2.
———. Letter to Samuel Bardsley, March 27, 1790. In *Letters* (Telford) 8:208–9.
———. Letter to Samuel Furly, February 21, 1756. In *Letters* (Telford) 3:164.
———. Letter to Samuel Sparrow, October 9, 1773. In *Letters* (Telford) 6:49–50.
———. Letter to Samuel Walker, November 20, 1755. In *Letters* (Telford) 3:152–53.
———. Letter to Samuel Wesley Jr., November 23, 1736. In *Letters* (Telford) 1:207–10.
———. Letter to Sarah Wesley, March 20, 1788. In *Letters* (Telford) 8:49.
———. Letter to Sophia Cooke, June 20, 1786. In *Letters* (Telford) 7:334–35.
———. Letter to the Printer of the *Dublin Chronicle*, June 2, 1789. In *Letters* (Telford) 8:139–43.
———. Letter to the Rev. Thomas Hartley, March 27, 1764. In *Letters* (Telford) 4:234–35.
———. Letter to Thomas Adam, October 31, 1755. In *Letters* (Telford) 3:149–52.
———. Letter to William Black, July 13, 1783. In *Letters* (Telford) 7:182–83.
———. Letter to William Black, March, 1790. In *Letters* (Telford) 8:204.
———. Letter to William Black, November 26, 1786. In *Letters* (Telford) 7:352.
———. Letter to William Orpe, November 13, 1765. In *Letters* (Telford) 4:315.
———. Letter to William Percival, February 17, 1787. In *Letters* (Telford) 7:369–70.
———. Letter to William Thom, June 21, 1790. In *Letters* (Telford) 8:223–24.

———. *The Letters of the Rev. John Wesley.* Edited by John Telford. 8 vols. London: Epworth, 1931.

———. "Manuscript Diaries Editorial Note." In *Works* (Bicentennial) 23:431.

———. *Minutes of the Methodist Conferences.* London: Mason, 1862.

———. *A Plain Account of Christian Perfection.* In *Works* (Jackson) 11:366–446.

———. *Prayers for Children.* In *Works* (Jackson) 11:259–72.

———. Preface to *Explanatory Notes on the Old Testament.* In *Works* (Jackson) 14:246–53.

———. Preface to "John Wesley's Spirituality: A Collection of Forms of Prayer for Every Day in the Week." In *John and Charles Wesley: Selected Prayers, Hymns, Journal Notes, Sermons, Letters and Treatises*, edited by Frank Whaling, 77–79. Classics of Western Spirituality. New York: Paulist, 1981.

———. "The Principles of a Methodist Farther Explained." In *Works* (Jackson) 8:414–81.

———. "Reasons Against a Separation from the Church of England." In *Works* (Jackson) 13:225–32.

———. "Sermon 5—Justification by Faith." In *Works* (Jackson) 5:53–64.

———. "Sermon 6—The Righteousness of Faith." In *Works* (Jackson) 5:65–76.

———. "Sermon 9—The Spirit of Bondage and Adoption." In *Works* (Jackson) 5:98–111.

———. "Sermon 10—The Witness of the Spirit, I." In *Works* (Jackson) 5:111–23.

———. "Sermon 16—The Means of Grace." In *Works* (Jackson) 5:185–201.

———. "Sermon 21—Sermon on the Mount, I." In *Works* (Jackson) 5:247–61.

———. "Sermon 23—The Sermon on the Mount, III." In *Works* (Jackson) 5:278–94.

———. "Sermon 25—Sermon on the Mount, V." In *Works* (Jackson) 5:310–27.

———. "Sermon 26—Sermon on the Mount, VI." In *Works* (Jackson) 5:327–43.

———. "Sermon 27—Sermon on the Mount, VII." In *Works* (Jackson) 5:343–60.

———. "Sermon 28—Sermon on the Mount, VIII." In *Works* (Jackson) 5:361–77.

———. "Sermon 30—Sermon on the Mount, X." In *Works* (Jackson) 5:393–404.

———. "Sermon 38—A Caution Against Bigotry." In *Works* (Jackson) 5:479–92.

———. "Sermon 39—Catholic Spirit." In *Works* (Jackson) 5:492–504.

———. "Sermon 41—Wandering Thoughts." In *Works* (Jackson) 6:23–32.

———. "Sermon 42—Satan's Devices." In *Works* (Jackson) 6:33–43.

———. "Sermon 43—The Scripture Way of Salvation." In *Works* (Jackson) 6:43–54.

———. "Sermon 46—The Wilderness State." In *Works* (Jackson) 6:77–91.

———. "Sermon 59—God's Love to Fallen Man." In *Works* (Jackson) 6:231–40.

———. "Sermon 67—On Divine Providence." In *Works* (Jackson) 6:313–25.

———. "Sermon 71—Of Good Angels." In *Works* (Jackson) 6:361–70.

———. "Sermon 76—On Perfection." In *Works* (Jackson) 6:411–24.

———. "Sermon 77—Spiritual Worship." In *Works* (Jackson) 6:424–35.

———. "Sermon 83—On Patience." In *Works* (Jackson) 6:484–92.

———. "Sermon 85—On Working Out Our Own Salvation." In *Works* (Jackson) 6:506–13.

———. "Sermon 89—The More Excellent Way." In *Works* (Jackson) 7:26–37.

———. "Sermon 105—On Conscience." In *Works* (Jackson) 7:186–94.

———. "Sermon 110—On the Discoveries of Faith." In *Works* (Jackson) 7:231–38.

———. "Sermon 114—The Unity of the Divine Being." In *Works* (Jackson) 7:264–73.

———. "Sermon 116—Causes of the Inefficacy of Christianity." In *Works* (Jackson) 7:281–90.

———. "Sermon 117—On Knowing Christ After the Flesh." In *Works* (Jackson) 7:291–96.

———. "Sermon 118—On a Single Eye." In *Works* (Jackson) 7:297–305.

———. "A Short Account of the School in Kingswood." In *Works* (Jackson) 13:285.

———. *The Sunday Service of the Methodists in North America*. London: 1788.

———. *The Works of John Wesley*. Edited by Thomas Jackson. 14 vols. London: Wesleyan Methodist Book Room, 1829-31. Repr., Grand Rapids: Zondervan, 1955.

Wesley, Martha. Letter to John Wesley, January 10, 1730. In *John Wesley's In-Correspondence (1724–30)*, Wesley Works Editorial Project, 107–8. https://wesleyworks.wordpress.com/wp-content/uploads/2023/09/jw-in-correspondence-1724-30.pdf.

Wesley, Samuel, Jr. Letter to John Wesley, April 16, 1739. In *John Wesley's In-Correspondence (1736–40)*, Wesley Works Editorial Project, 113–14. https://wesleyworks.wordpress.com/wp-content/uploads/2023/09/jw-in-correspondence-1736-40.pdf.

Wesley, Samuel, Sr. Letter to John Wesley, January 26, 1725. In *John Wesley's In-Correspondence (1724–30)*, Wesley Works Editorial Project, 7–8. https://wesleyworks.wordpress.com/wp-content/uploads/2023/09/jw-in-correspondence-1724-30.pdf.

———. Letter to John Wesley, July 14, 1725. In *John Wesley's In-Correspondence (1724–30)*, Wesley Works Editorial Project, 21–22. https://wesleyworks.wordpress.com/wp-content/uploads/2023/09/jw-in-correspondence-1724-30.pdf.

———. Letter to John Wesley, March 17, 1725. In *John Wesley's In-Correspondence (1724–30)*, Wesley Works Editorial Project, 13. https://wesleyworks.wordpress.com/wp-content/uploads/2023/09/jw-in-correspondence-1724-30.pdf.

———. Letter to John Wesley, September 7, 1725. In *John Wesley's In-Correspondence (1724–30)*, Wesley Works Editorial Project, 33. https://wesleyworks.wordpress.com/wp-content/uploads/2023/09/jw-in-correspondence-1724-30.pdf.

———. Letter to John Wesley, September 28, 1730. In *Letters* (Telford) 1:125–26.

Wesley, Susanna. Letter to John Wesley, July 24, 1732. In *Works* (Jackson) 1:387–93.

———. Letter to John Wesley, June 8, 1725. In *John Wesley's In-Correspondence (1724–30)*, Wesley Works Editorial Project, 18–20. https://wesleyworks.wordpress.com/wp-content/uploads/2023/09/jw-in-correspondence-1724-30.pdf.

———. *Susanna Wesley: The Complete Writings*. Edited by Charles Wallace Jr. New York: Oxford University Press, 1997.

Whitefield, George. Letter to John Wesley, July 2, 1739. In *John Wesley's In-Correspondence (1736–40)*, Wesley Works Editorial Project, 133. https://wesleyworks.wordpress.com/wp-content/uploads/2023/09/jw-in-correspondence-1736-40.pdf.

Willis, Thomas. Letter to John Wesley, November 13, 1744. In *John Wesley's In-Correspondence (1741–45)*, Wesley Works Editorial Project, 191–93. https://wesleyworks.wordpress.com/wp-content/uploads/2023/09/jw-in-correspondence-1741-45.pdf.

www.ingramcontent.com/pod-product-compliance
Lightning Source LLC
Chambersburg PA
CBHW050817160426
43192CB00010B/1797